FLAT TRACK FASHION:
THE ROLLER DERBY LOOK BOOK

Acknowledgements

With special thanks to Robert Fiehn, Susan James for making it all possible, Danny Bourne for fabulous photography, Saffron Stocker and Sutchinda Thompson for fantastic design, Hayley Yeeles for being a star, Emily Clarke and Martha Singh Jennings for their amazing hair styling, Louise O'Neill and Erica Schlegel for beautiful make-up, Jerry Seltzer, Joe Nardone, James Vannurden at the National Museum of Roller Skating for the historical photos, Jason Ruffell, Amanda Renee, Antonio Soares, Nestor Benitez, Sleaze Machine, Neal Humphris, Timothy Moxley, Andreas Koch, Joe Schwartz, Jules Doyle, Asa Frye, Nadia Caffesse, Hana Schlesinger, Nadine Windberg, Denise Krause, Felicia Graham, Krystin Bogan, Ray Lowe Studios and Paul Herring for all the fantastic photographs. Kit Kat Power, Dom Holmes, Pivotstar, Wicked Skatewear, Riedell skates, fiveonfive magazine, Atom Wheels, Bones Bearings, London Rollergirls, London Rockin' Rollers, Kokeshi Roller Dolls, Stockhom Roller Derby, Berlin Bombshells, Buenos Aires Roller Derby, Roller Derby of Korea, Northside Roller Derby, Richter City Roller Derby, North Pole Babes in Toyland, Republic of Korea Derby, Gotham Girls Roller Derby and Ladies of Hell Town for all their help, logo designs and contributions, and to all the beautiful rollergirl models.

First published in 2012 by A & C Black,
an imprint of Bloomsbury Publishing Plc.
50 Bedford Square,
London WC1B 3DP
www.acblack.com

Text copyright © Ellen Parnavelas 2012
Images copyright © individual photographers as credited in photo captions

CIP Catalogue records for this book are available from the British Library and the US Library of Congress.

Publisher: Susan James
Copy editor: Julian Beecroft
Book design by Saffron Stocker
Cover design by Sutchinda Thompson

Front cover image: Suzy Hotrod of Gotham Girls Roller Derby, USA. Photo provided by Getty.
Back cover images:
Top: Red N Roll, Kit Kat Power, Bloody Valentine and Sin D. Doll, London Rockin' Rollers, UK. Photo by Danny Bourne.
Bottom left: Trippi Hit Run, The Good, the Bad and the Gorgeous, Berlin Bombshells, Germany. Photo by Mis Van D.
Bottom right: Disorder Lee, London Rockin Rollers, UK. Photo by Paul Herring.
Front flap: Boba Fetish, Tiger Bay Brawlers, Wales. Photo by Jason Ruffell.
Back flap: Ladies of Hell Town, Sao Paolo, Brazil. Photo by Daniel Caetano.

ISBN 978-1-4081-5501-1

FLAT TRACK FASHION:
THE ROLLER DERBY LOOK BOOK

Ellen Parnavelas

A & C Black · London

CONTENTS

Kit Kat Power of the London Rockin'
Rollers, UK. Photo by Danny Bourne.

FOREWORD

BY VIRGINIA 'CHEAP TRIXIE' EVANS

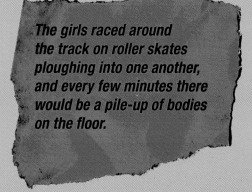

Virginia 'Cheap Trixie' Evans.
Photo by Nadia Cafesse.

FLASHBACK: 11th January 2003, Austin Music Hall, downtown Austin, Texas. I was 23 and coming out of a pretty rough breakup, so my best friend Rosie insisted on getting me out of my apartment one night. On this particular night she was determined on dragging me to the first annual Star of Texas Tattoo convention that was being held in downtown Austin. The entertainment that night was a live performance by Austin's roller derby girls and local band the Riverboat Gamblers! I knew nothing about roller derby, old or new, but I knew the Riverboat Gamblers rocked so I slipped into something presentable and hopped in my car. Little did I know that after the night was over my life would never be the same again. You see, Rosie had already seen the rollergirls and was completely determined to become one herself. However, she wanted a buddy to come along for the ride.

That night, I watched Bad Girl Good Woman (BGGW) Productions present a roller derby bout. The Rhinestone Cowgirls and The Holy Rollers competed on a small flat oval track that was uncomfortably nestled between six concrete pillars that were covered in mattresses and floor mats. The girls raced around the track on roller skates ploughing into one another, and every few minutes there would be a pile-up of bodies on the floor. All you could see in the mound of girls were a few flying, tattooed fists and flailing, fishnet-covered legs here and there. It was like watching a punk rock version of the Tasmanian Devil cartoon. These girls were out of control!

The majority of the skaters were tattooed and appeared to be tough as nails. I recognized a lot of them from the Red River district of Austin. This area is known for some of the best live underground rock music you can see in a three-block span. It was and still is a rock'n'roll artery for the Austin music scene and it became the life source of the modern-day roller derby revival. The skaters' outfits, or should I dare say 'uniforms', definitely paid a homage to their stomping grounds and their names were punked up to suit their respected teams. The Holy Rollers had names like Strawberry and Miss Conduct and wore torn-up fishnets and Catholic-school skirts that were definitely not the regulation

length of any Catholic school skirts I have ever seen. The Rhinestone Cowgirls wore cute red western shirts that were tied up to show their midriffs and ripped-up denim bottoms that looked pretty worn in. And with names like Rolletta Lynn and Barbie Crash you can tell that they were a little bit country with a bunch of rock'n'roll.

After that night was over I couldn't tell if I was deathly afraid of these girls or completely in love. The next few weeks were filled with my friend Rosie trying to convince me to try out with her at the end of the month and dragging me to Playland Skate Center's adult skate night to practise. She thought I would be perfect for the league, but I was still to be convinced that I had what it took to roll with these chicks. So Rosie did what any smart woman would do to get what she wants – she brought in the big guns. One of my co-workers was a rollergirl by the name of Bettie Rage. Rosie filled her in with her intent to try out and her intent to bring me along with her. Now, I had not one but two very convincing ladies at my desk on a daily basis poking at me to at least just go to tryouts. So I did, and Cheap Trixie was born.

The girls raced around the track on roller skates ploughing into one another, and every few minutes there would be a pile-up of bodies on the floor.

PRESENT DAY: 2011, finishing up my 9th season as a member of the Hustlers for the Texas Rollergirls. Fashion in the early days of roller derby was very different from what it is today. When I joined roller derby in early 2003 I was placed on the new 5th team, The Hustlers. And not too long after that Bad Girl Good Woman Productions split into a banked track league and a flat track league. I stayed with the flat track league, which became the Texas Rollergirls. With the split the flat track teams became: The Hell Marys, The Honkytonk Heartbreakers, The Hot

Rod Honeys and The Hustlers.

With all the league changes came changes to our uniforms. The Hustlers, being the new team on the block, were the only team able to keep our name and team colours after the split. And since we had already been working on our new threads, we just kept doing what we were doing, which was spending hours upon hours at Hissy Fit's house, pinning and sewing down less than cooperative purple and silver spandex. But the other teams had a rough job. They had to redefine the look of their team while keeping within the themes. But back then redefining was much different from what it is now. True, the teams had themes, but their uniforms were far from UNI-formed.

Back in the 'good ol' days' skaters couldn't just order their uniforms – well, we could, but let's say the options out there were a little dull for the creative types that formed our league. So each skater was given guidelines for making their uniform rather than group ordering information. Everyone was encouraged to add their own flare and personal style to their get-up, as long as they kept within the overall team theme and colours. Skater personas were encouraged to be over-the-top, and their uniforms were meant to express their alter egos. It wasn't just a uniform; it was a statement; one which immediately conveyed the message that you were a rollergirl for your team and not any other. However, changes were on the horizon in the form of the new purple team, The Hustlers. We were to be one of the first teams in the league to have an actual uniformed look to our 'uniforms'. I blame the spandex.

For the most part today's rollergirl look is some distance from the look of the past. But I see a transition happening that is much like the one I saw when the Hustlers first took to the floor at their inaugural game. Of course, there are still the campy and edgy styles of uniform that encourage personal flare and give a nod to our punk-rock roots, but now there are teams that have completely eliminated skater names, and have uniforms

that make it almost completely impossible for you to tell one skater from another. The fun, whimsical personas and alter egos of the girls are disappearing, and being replaced with a more professional and serious athletic girl that just glows 'SERIOUS SPORT'. There are now companies that specialize in roller derby uniforms, and the days of uniform guidelines and sewing parties are gradually becoming a thing of the past. Uniqueness and personal style are slowly going away to a certain degree. This is not a bad thing, as it shows how our sport is growing and maturing into something that could never have been imagined in 2003. But despite all these changes, I will always feel that no matter what we mature into, roller derby will always be a sport that is different in the way its players dress. At our roots we will always have the edgy, rock'n'roll creative types that hold the many mature individual branches together.

> *Everyone was encouraged to add their own flare and personal style to their get-up, as long as they kept within the overall team theme and colours. Skater personas were encouraged to be over-the-top, and their uniforms were meant to express their alter egos.*

Virginia 'Cheap Trixie' Evans skating with the Hustlers, Texas Rollergirls. Photo by Felicia Graham.

INTRODUCTION

Roller derby has been present in various forms throughout the 20th century, but in the last 10 years it has experienced a revival, taking its popularity to highs never achieved before. Now dubbed as 'the world's fastest growing sport', there are new leagues starting up all over the world, from its original homeland in the US to nations far and wide throughout Europe, Asia, Australasia and Latin America. Roller derby has become a truly global phenomenon and it is not uncommon for crowds at games to reach up to 6,000 spectators.

Flat track roller derby is a game played on an oval track by two teams of five players. In each team, four of the players are 'blockers' and one is the 'jammer'. The blockers from both teams skate around the track together, forming a 'pack', with the two jammers starting behind them. The jammer is a racing skater whose job it is to race through the pack and lap the players on the opposing team, scoring points for every opposing player passed. The blockers in the pack try to stop the opposing jammer from getting through the pack while also trying to help their jammer through by blocking the opposing players.

At this point you may be asking why this sport has become so popular right now, at this point in the 21st century. Well, the recent roller derby revival began in Austin, Texas in 2000 with a group of women with one foot in the alternative music scene. There are now many men playing roller derby, but in 2000 it started with just the women. These pioneers decided to form the first DIY, grassroots-operated flat track roller derby league for women, and many others followed suit. It soon became apparent that many women were looking for an opportunity to express themselves, form communities, be competitive and athletic, and play a tough, full-contact sport as men do. The roller derby revival presented an opportunity for them to do all of these things without men, such that flat track roller derby became a contact sport that women could call their own.

Historically, women have always been part of roller derby. Many of the 20th century's star players were women, with the likes of Gerry Murray, Ann Calvello and Joan Weston becoming public heroes and household names. In the original Transcontinental Roller Derby of the 1930s, and throughout the 20th century, it was played by both men and women. It was one of the first sports where women took centre stage and were paid as professional athletes.

Suzy Hotrod of Gotham Girls Roller Derby, USA. Photo by Joe Schwartz.

Violet Attack of the Birmingham Blitz Dames, UK. Photo by Jason Ruffell.

Brutal Strudel of the Atlanta Rollergirls, USA, in her red and blue uniform. Photo by Timothy Moxley.

It is in no way surprising that, in the 21st century, where modern life places high demands of various kinds on women, that they wanted a sport to call their own. In playing roller derby, women found that they didn't have to live up to all of the unrealistic expectations placed on them by society and could even contradict them. They could be who they are and do something for themselves as complex, multifaceted individuals, not oversimplified by society's expectations.

Roller derby is a culture that embraces all backgrounds, styles and abilities. The motto of the Women's Flat Track Derby Association (WFTDA) best sums up the spirit of it: 'Real, Strong, Athletic, Revolutionary'. It is a culture through which women and increasing numbers of men learn, develop, achieve and express themselves through the medium of sport. But it is more than that: there are countless stories that begin, 'Roller derby changed my life . . .'

Roller derby isn't just a sport; it's a way of life. For those who play, it reaches into every aspect of their lives, from social life to diet to politics, personal relationships and, of course, fashion. There is a place for everyone in roller derby, as it embraces people from all backgrounds, from lifelong athletes to first-time sports lovers.

Fashion has always been a big part of roller derby, which is a medium of self-expression as well as being a sport. There are now many retailers providing clothing specifically for roller derby skaters including Wicked Skatewear, Pivotstar and Derby Skinz, to name but a few. Even in the early 20th century, the fashion aspect of roller derby was always emphasized, from the famous 'hair bows' worn by Gerry Murray to the signature multicoloured hair and tattoos worn by Ann Calvello, skaters were always remembered for their signature 'look'. Although it is a sport, it also has its roots firmly planted in spectacle and performance, and the look has always been part of the surrounding culture. From the beginning of the revival, a lot of emphasis

was placed on team uniforms and outfits, with rollergirls creating alter egos. It was a competitive sport where women could be creative with fashion and be tough and sexy, feminine and athletic all at the same time.

As with the wide range in athletic experience, there is room for all styles. From pin-up and vintage looks to punk and goth, and from simple sportswear to nu-rave neon, though teammates are often unified by an overall uniform design or colour scheme, there is plenty of room for individual style and interpretation. Not all derby girls fit into the stereotype of the tough-talking punk chick: skaters come from all professions and backgrounds, and a full spectrum of personalities can be found on the track. This is reflected in the range of fashion styles on display.

As the sport has grown and developed, a greater emphasis has been placed on its athleticism, so that more and more functional sportswear has been adopted. However, there are plenty of rollergirls out there displaying fabulous boutfits, with fishnet-clad thighs and plenty of tattoos. Some people would argue that the fashion detracts from the seriousness and athleticism of the sport, but I think there is plenty of room for fashion and sport to coexist and be taken seriously. This book is a celebration of roller derby fashion past and present, a catalogue of the style, sass and skates from all over the world. I hope as the sport continues to grow that the culture of creative self-expression and individual style can grow with it and continue to represent the spirit of roller derby.

Buenos Aires Roller Derby, Argentina. Photo by Nestor Benitez.

5,700 fans pack in to watch Rat City Rollergirls at Key Arena, Seattle, USA. Photo by Jules Doyle.

Blocking in style: Frida K.O., Cher Horror'itz and Mentally Un-Mayble, London Rollergirls Recreational League, UK. Photo by Danny Bourne.

RoboFlow, Red Ridin' Hoods,
Rocky Mountian Rollergirls, USA.
Photo by Amanda Renee, Wicked
Shamrock Photography.

THE HISTORY OF ROLLER DERBY

Roller derby is currently experiencing a new wave of popularity since the most recent revival began in 2001. However, this fast and furious sport has a long and complex history and has been through many incarnations and phases of popularity over the course of the 20th century.

Vivian Johnson takes a hard hit, 1948. Photo provided by Getty.

Roller skating sports date back to the 19th century, when the first roller skates had not long been invented. The growing popularity of roller skating during the late 1880s led to the development of roller skating endurance races. The very first race on roller skates took place in Illinois, when Victor W. Clough skated 100 miles in approximately 10 hours. This was soon followed by the first roller skating marathon, which took place in 1885 at Madison Square Garden in New York City. The event was a six-day skating marathon where men from all over the world entered the contest to see how many miles they could skate in a day. William Donovan was the winner of the competition. However, tragically, he died a week after the race and the cause of his death was thought to have been aggravated by his participation in the marathon. Another participant, Joseph Cohen also died shortly after competing due to meningitis brought on by overexertion.

Following these unfortunate fatalities, roller skating as a sport was condemned by the public as a mad, bad and dangerous vice. This sudden reputation brought it to an end as a public sport for almost the next 50 years, with only a few similar endurance races taking place every now and then. However, roller skating races and marathons became very popular again during the Great Depression after the Wall Street Crash of 1929. During this period, endurance races of various types became favourites of the public as unemployment was high and people needed distractions to take their minds off the bleak economic outlook.

Leo Seltzer was the inventor of the original roller derby. A sports promoter during the 1930s, he made fast cash by inventing new and crazy forms of entertainment for the unemployed workforce of America. Schemes of his that preceded the advent of roller derby included walkathons, ice-sitting contests, vaudeville comedians and unusual public wedding ceremonies. After realizing the popularity of roller skating among the American public, Seltzer started up the Transcontinental Roller Derby in Chicago in 1933, with its debut game held at the Chicago Coliseum in 1935 in front of more than 20,000 spectators.

The Transcontinental Roller Derby was a skating marathon that ran for approximately seven weeks from midday until 2am every day, in which 25 male/female couples would try to skate 57,000 laps of a flat track that covered roughly the distance from New York to San Diego while their progress was tracked on a map of the famous transcontinental highway, Route 66. The popularity of this debut event persuaded Leo Seltzer to take it on the road, so that he moved both his flat track and

> **Leo Seltzer was the inventor of the original roller derby. A sports promoter during the 1930s, he made fast cash by inventing new and crazy forms of entertainment for the unemployed workforce of America.**

Leo Seltzer, the founder of the original roller derby. Photo courtesy of Jerry Seltzer, provided by Joe Nardone.

Leo Seltzer, the founder of the original roller derby. Photo courtesy of Jerry Seltzer, provided by Joe Nardone.

AN APPRECIATION TO

LEO A. SELTZER

FOUNDER OF THE ROLLER DERBY

Gerry Murray fights off her opponents, 1948. Photo provided by Getty.

Raquel Welch in *Kansas City Bomber*, 1972, the classic roller derby film. Photo provided by Getty.

Rollergirls of the New York Chiefs representing America, 1953. Photo provided by Getty.

his skaters around the country to perform in front of audiences across the US.

Roller derby quickly evolved from a marathon into a full-contact action sport on wheels. The progression from the flat to the banked track added more speed to the races and a points system was introduced to the game. During these marathons, the skaters were required to stop and take part in short sprints that were known as 'jams', to increase the excitement for the viewers. According to popular belief, full contact was introduced to the sport when, at a marathon in 1937, one of the male skaters elbowed one of the other skaters and the crowd went wild. It was then that Leo Seltzer realized, with the help of journalist Damon Runyon, that what people wanted to watch was violence. Together they devised a new set of rules where hip-checks, full-body blocking and on-track violence prevailed. By the late 1930s, the sport had evolved from a marathon comprised of 25 couples to a competition between two rival teams. The rules of the game were constantly changing, but it was at this point that the concept of 'jammers' and 'blockers' was established, along with the main aim of the game, namely, to score points each time a member of the opposing team was passed.

At the time, the public believed that there were several teams competing around the country, but in truth Seltzer used the same

Jerry Seltzer. Photo courtesy of Jerry Seltzer, provided by Joe Nardone.

Skilful shoulder block thrown by Fuzzy Buchek, 1948. Photo provided by Getty.

group of skaters to form 'home' and 'away' teams in each city, to add rivalry and excitement to the game. The 'home' team were always either playing New York or Chicago, giving the illusion that there were numerous teams competing across the US. The two-team format, with five players on each team, survives to this day.

After a short lapse in popularity during the Second World War, roller derby again became immensely popular. In 1948 the sport was first aired on television and an impressive number of viewers tuned in to watch the action. The National Roller Derby League was formed, in which several teams competed, so that there was no longer a need for a pretend 'home' team. Television exposure increased its popularity, and in 1949 the National Roller Derby League world series drew in a crowd of 55,000 at Madison Square Garden. However, it is believed that what had made roller derby popular, television exposure, also caused its sudden decline. The public had seen too much and lost interest and, by 1951 roller derby had been dropped from the air by major network broadcasting. By 1953 the popularity of the sport had almost entirely evaporated, so Seltzer formed a new team, which toured around Europe for want of home fans.

In 1949 the National Roller Derby League World Series drew in a crowd of 55,000 at Madison Square Garden.

In 1958 Seltzer's roller derby was handed down to his son Jerry, who decided to revamp it and give it a new home in San Francisco. His league operated under the new name of San Francisco Bay Bombers and drew in new crowds with star skaters Ann Calvello, Joan Weston and Charlie O'Connell.

Roller derby maintained its popularity during the 1960s. With the invention of video, roller derby again raged across the airwaves, with recorded games being shown by smaller, independent television channels. The dangerous antics of the sport had captured the public's attention, and several films on the subject were released in the 1970s, including *Kansas City Bomber* starring Raquel Welch, and *Rollerball* starring James Caan.

This increasing popularity had also led to another, more theatrical version of roller derby, Roller Games, started by Bill Griffiths in southern California in the early 1960s. However, in the early 1970s this came to an end for various reasons, among which was the oil crisis of the

A skater from the New York Chiefs representing America in team uniform,1953. Photo provided by Getty.

Skater takes a tumble, 1953. Photo provided by Getty.

period, which prevented Seltzer's teams from travelling. By 1973 the sport's popularity had waned again and Jerry Seltzer was forced to close down his business.

There were several unsuccessful attempts to restart the sport during the 1970s and early '80s, and it did appear again briefly during the late '80s in the hybrid form of the RollerGames. This theatrical mutation of the sport was comprised of a skating track in the shape of a figure of eight where skaters committed staged acts of violence and attempted to push each other into an alligator pit. This sensationalist sister of roller derby was, however, very short-lived, disappearing after one series on late-night TV.

The flat track roller derby that the thousands who participate know and love today was born in Austin, Texas in 2000.

During the late 1990s the Seltzer family transformed roller derby into RollerJam, which was first viewed on television by the public in 1999. RollerJam traded in the old-fashioned quad skates for the newly popular in-line skates. It was an inline skating show based in Florida and shown on cable television. The game was played on a banked track by speed skaters and roller hockey players, embellished with dramatic stories from ProWrestling. However, something about this new format didn't quite work as audiences found it too staged and it lacked the athleticism of the earlier roller derby. However, though the popularity of RollerJam was only short-lived, it wasn't long before roller derby reinvented itself yet again.

The flat track roller derby that the thousands who participate know and love today was born in Austin, Texas in 2000. A member of the alternative music scene known as Devil Dan, later to be revealed as musician Daniel Eduardo Policarpo, had the idea of launching a roller derby for the feisty women of Austin. His vision was for a circus-like show with midgets and fire twirlers performing in a theatre. Dan's idea was very popular amongst the locals and, by early 2001, he had signed up about twenty rough and ready women to participate, including Rachelle Moore, later to be known as Sparkle Plenty, and April Ritzenthaler, later to be known as La Muerta. Devil Dan devised four teams: the Rhinestone Cowgirls, captained by Anya Jack aka Hot Lips Dolly; the Holy Rollers, captained by Amanda Harrison aka Miss Information; the Putas del Fuego, captained by April Ritzenthaler aka La Muerta; and the Hellcats, captained by Nancy Haggarty aka Iron

Jerry Seltzer with Ann Calvello, the 'demon of derby'. Photo courtesy of Jerry Seltzer, provided by Joe Nardone.

Raquel Welch in *Kansas City Bomber*, 1972, the classic roller derby film. Photo provided by Getty.

Maiden. They made plans, had discussions, held fundraisers and time passed but still no one had started skating.

According to the fable, Devil Dan suddenly disappeared and the newly appointed captains of the teams took it upon themselves to get organized. Nicknamed the SheEOs, this group of women got into gear and started up the first female flat track roller derby league. They formed Bad Girl Good Woman Productions and, with the help of the other new recruits, pooled their skills to teach each other how to skate, play the game and get themselves physically ready for the athleticism of the sport. Sparkle Plenty captained the rules committee and together they adapted the rules of the sport to make a new set of rules for women's flat track roller derby. The flat track was adopted as there was no way the Texas skaters could afford to buy and install a banked track in the same style as the roller derby of the past. They adapted the measurements of the old-style banked track, and, using a CAD programme, calculated what the dimensions would be if the track was laid flat.

> *They started up the first DIY women-only roller derby league, complete with sexy and stylish uniforms, witty names and alter egos, fierce athleticism and lashings of attitude.*

These women had taken it into their own hands to start the grassroots league they had dreamed of. With Devil Dan out of the picture, they started up the first DIY women-only roller derby league, complete with sexy and stylish uniforms, witty names and alter egos, fierce athleticism and lashings of attitude.

By early 2002, the league had 45 players all of whom had volunteered to help run different parts of it, establishing the tradition of the skaters running the league themselves. They played their first public bout on 23rd June 2002 for an audience of friends and family. The bout was a success and the league had finally established itself.

In early 2003, halfway through the first season, a lot of the skaters in the league became dissatisfied with the way it was being run. They felt that it was becoming more of a commercial operation led by the SheEOs and wanted more control and an equal system of voting for how the league was managed.

In the original roller derbies of the 1930s and 1940s, the skaters

Roger Schroeder on the banked track, 1953. Photo provided by Getty.

Bill Reynolds, 1948. Photo provided by Getty.

Dewitt Charles of the San Francisco Bay Bombers, takes out Buzz Sanders of the New York Chiefs, 1967. Photo provided by Getty.

were professional, paid athletes. Indeed, according to Jerry Seltzer, roller derby was the first sport ever to establish profit sharing for its participants. In the original roller derby all receipts were totalled after the end of the run in a particular city (usually two to four weeks) and divided among the participants and staff. Usually the less-popular skaters would get about $25 each, while the more popular could get $100, which in addition to food and accommodation costs made for a very reasonable salary. By the 1960s, top skaters were being paid $40,000–60,000 a year, and until the roller derby shut down in 1973 the players received anywhere from $5,000 to $70,000 a year. However, the roller derby was not owned or run by the skaters themselves, but was a commercial enterprise owned by Seltzer.

In early 2003 in Austin it looked as though the SheEOs leading Bad Girl Good Woman Productions were taking steps towards making their league a registered business, and the skaters were not happy. This created a lot of tension within the league and eventually led the skaters to revolt. They wanted to run a grassroots, skater-owned

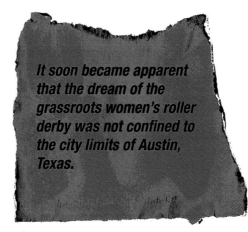

It soon became apparent that the dream of the grassroots women's roller derby was not confined to the city limits of Austin, Texas.

league themselves and they decided to take action and do something about it. The original members of Bad Girl Good Woman Productions then divided into two leagues: the Texas Rollergirls and the TXRD Lonestar Rollergirls. Bad Girl Good Woman Productions under the leadership of the SheEOs was left with 15 of their original members, who formed the TXRD Lonestar Rollergirls. The new TXRD Lonestar league differentiated itself from the original league by purchasing an original Bay Bombers banked track to skate on. The two leagues continue operating along these separate lines to this day.

It soon became apparent that the dream of the grassroots women's roller derby was not confined to the city limits of Austin, Texas. Shortly after the Texas split, Denise Grimes aka Ivanna S. Pankin, a painter from the punk scene in Phoenix Arizona, started work on forming the Arizona Roller Derby. They were up and running by August 2003 and played their first bout that November. Nearby, in the town of Tuscon, a former truck-stop waitress who was to become Kim Sin heard about the Arizona Roller Derby and decided to start her own league, which held its first rollergirl recruitment meeting in December 2003. In April 2004 Tucson Roller Derby played their first bout against Arizona Roller Derby.

Since 2003, flat track roller derby leagues have sprung up at a pace that's as fast and furious as the sport itself. One of the first was the LA Derby Dolls, inaugurated by a sculptor by the name of Rebecca Ninburg, later to be known as Demoliscious, and Wendy Templeton aka Thora Zeen; herself a painter. In Brooklyn, New York, Karin Bruce aka Chassis Crass, started up the Gotham Girls Roller Derby League. Celia Fate started up the Carolina Rollegirls, who were soon followed by the Rat City Rollergirls of Seattle, the Kansas City Roller Warriors, the Mad Rollin' Dolls in Wisconsin, the Rose City Rollers in Portland, the Rocky Mountain Rollergirls in Denver, the Bay Area Rollergirls in San Francisco, the Minnesota Rollergirls in Minneapolis and the Providence Rollergirls in Rhode Island.

The United Leagues Coalition, or ULC, was then formed to establish a cohesive governing body for the sport charged with the responsibility of drawing up a standardized set of rules and organizing competitions between leagues. Beginning in 2004 with a mission statement promising to facilitate the development of athletic ability, sportswomanship, and goodwill among member leagues, according to their website, their governing philosophy is 'by the skaters, for the skaters'. They held their first meeting in 2005, welcoming any leagues who wanted to join to become members. This led 30 leagues to join forces, and at the same time the decision was taken to rename the organization the Women's Flat Track Derby Association (now known as WFTDA), the organization at the head of the sport today.

WFTDA is the central governing body behind women's flat track roller derby. WFTDA is responsible for setting the rules of the game, establishing seasons of play and safety guidelines, and organizing officially sanctioned competitions among members. Annual championship games are held based on these competitions, while a ranking system of member leagues has also been established. In September 2006 WFTDA opened its doors to new members and has continued to do so ever since. There are now 124 member leagues and 76 apprentice leagues.

Since 2003, flat track roller derby leagues have sprung up at a pace that's as fast and furious as the sport itself.

Fuzzy Bucheck in action, 1948. Photo provided by Getty.

The WFTDA member leagues are divided into four regions: US East, US West, US North Central and US South Central. Two new regions, Canada and Europe, have recently been formed due to the rapid growth of roller derby outside the US. However, these regions have yet to be developed, and until they establish more members teams in those regions will compete in their closest US region for rankings and tournaments. Every year, each region holds a tournament involving the top 10 teams from that region, and the top three teams in each region go through to compete in the annual WFTDA Championship.

Although WFTDA is the most established governing body in the sport today, there are many leagues operating and competing that are not members of WFTDA. For instance, there are several other organizations that have recently been established for other forms of roller derby. The Men's Roller Derby Association, MRDA, was established for the increasing number of male leagues and teams that have started up in recent years. The Old School Derby Association, OSDA, was started in 2007 for a version of roller derby based on earlier forms of the game played predominantly on a banked track, though this organization caters to men's, women's and mixed-sex groups playing on flat or banked tracks. The OSDA Professional League established its first team in 2010, playing on a banked track. The major banked track leagues formed the World Organisation of Roller Derby, WORD, in 2009, with

rules compatible with those of WFTDA. The Renegade Rollergirls also formed in 2004, playing a form of roller derby with no referees or penalties and on a variety of surfaces, outdoor and indoor.

Roller derby has flung itself far and wide and today has spread internationally like wildfire. There are now over 1000 established leagues across the globe in places throughout the US, Australia, New Zealand, Latin America, Asia and Europe. The sport's development has been vastly enabled by contemporary online resources and social-networking sites, and derby communities around the world have developed a very strong online presence. It is now the fastest-growing sport in the world, but who knows what the future holds.

Toughie Brasuhn gets tough with opponent, 1953. Photo provided by Getty.

UNIFORMS AND LOGOS

Uniforms and logos have been an integral part of the recent roller derby revival since 2001 and are very much a distinguishing feature of the sport an its culture. Every league and the teams within it are defined by their unique and specially designed logo and uniform so they can be distinguished from their opponents on the track.

Whipity Pow jamming for the
Dooms Daisies and She Who
Cannot be Named jamming
for the Red Ridin' Hoods,
Rocky Mountain Rollergirls,
USA. Photo by Amanda Renee,
Wicked Shamrock Photography.

UNIFORMS

Every roller derby league is comprised of several teams, usually a minimum of two depending on how many skaters are in the league. These teams compete publicly in 'bouts', the derby name for games or matches. It is now not uncommon in the US for audiences to reach 3000, or even 4000, people. Within a league, each team is unified by their look and very often each will have its own uniquely designed uniform, worn for competing in public bouts. Leagues often have a 'travel team' made up of their star players for competing in regional tournaments, and they too have their own unique uniform in league colours.

A team uniform can be anything from a simple T-shirt to a specially designed dress or tunic complete with matching hotpants or skirts, helmets and make-up. There are a million ways in which teams get creative with their uniforms, from the orange and black stripes of Wales's very own Tiger Bay Brawlers, to the Day-Glo green and neon-

There are a million ways in which teams get creative with their uniforms, from the orange and black stripes of Wales's very own Tiger Bay Brawlers, to the Day-Glo green and neon-pink style of the Montreal New Skids on the Block

pink style of the Montreal New Skids on the Block, complete with raver-style shades worn in the team profile pictures on their website. Uniforms are often influenced by rockabilly, punk, burlesque, goth and vintage fashions. However, the creativity of fashion in team uniforms differs from one league to another, as some leagues prefer to keep it simple and to emphasize the athleticism of the sport. Some leagues, on the other hand, embrace the styling of uniforms and the fashion side of roller derby.

Historically, roller derby teams wore matching uniforms on the track, even back in the 1930s when the sport began. During this period fashions were a lot more conservative, but roller derby uniforms were often form-fitting, figure-hugging outfits similar to those worn today. They often consisted of matching sports tops and high-waisted shorts, much like today's favourite roller derby garment: hotpants. These were worn with fitted sports leggings underneath, reinforced with leather around the knee area for added protection.

Fabulous fluro: Montreal Roller Derby's New Skids on the Block at half-time. Photo by Jules Doyle.

Ecchi Killer of the Harbour Grudges, London Rollergirls, UK wears nautical themed uniform. Photo by Neal 'Hassle Brad' Humphris.

Keeping it animal: Boba Fetish
of the Tiger Bay Brawlers, UK.
Photo by Jason Ruffell.

Red n Roll, Kit Kat Power, Bloody Valentine and Sin D. Doll of London Rockin' Rollers, London, UK. Photo by Danny Bourne.

From the beginning of the roller derby revival in 2001, the team uniforms were integral to the sport and its growing culture.

Uniform styles are often designed according to team name, creating a running theme: for example, the LA Derby Dolls' Sirens Derby Squad bad-cop police-squadron-style uniform in dark blue, complete with badge; or the London Rollergirls' Ultraviolent Femmes with their uniform inspired by Stanley Kubrick's legendary film *A Clockwork Orange*. Their team colours are white and acid-green complete with the logo of an ultraviolent's face adorned with bowler hat and painted-on eyelashes in the style of Alex and his droogs in Kubrick's film. The Atlanta Rollergirls' team, the Sake Tuyas, have a distinctly Japanese-themed uniform, wearing white tunics with kimono-

Uniform styles are often designed according to team name, creating a running theme

style necklines, with many players adding personal touches to this look.

Team names and uniforms are also often linked with a team's 'skate-out song'. The 'skate-out song' is a victorious awe-inspiring anthem that a team uses to introduce themselves to the crowd at the beginning of a bout. As the music echoes around the track and through the crowd, the team skates out in a line and makes a few laps of the track, often with each player skating out in front of the line and waving to the audience while the announcer introduces them by skate name and number.

The London Rollergirls again are a good example of this as their travel team London Brawling seem to have constructed their identity around their skate-out song: 'London Calling' by The Clash. Their pink and black uniform with pink and black Union Jack logos echoes the style of the cover art for the album Never Mind the Bollocks, the seminal album by those other punk gods The Sex Pistols. A 'skate-out song' often completes an ensemble and unifies a theme.

Although a team's look is brought together by a uniform, the customization of uniforms by individuals is always encouraged. Rarely will you see two rollergirls that look identical, even if they are on the same team. With the right know-how a simple team t-shirt with logo can be adapted into a highly individual fashion creation. Sleeves are often hacked off, necklines slashed, ribbons, safety pins and other adornments added, and, for those who like to get creative with a sewing machine, ruching at the sides, corset-style lacing and any number of bespoke innovations are possible. Many skaters have their own unique uniform customization ritual and will rarely, if ever, wear a uniform t-shirt in its original form.

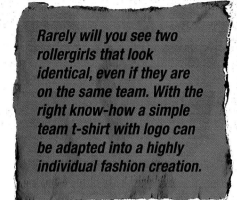

Rarely will you see two rollergirls that look identical, even if they are on the same team. With the right know-how a simple team t-shirt with logo can be adapted into a highly individual fashion creation.

Another great way to customize a uniform is to accessorize. That's right, fashion's first rule of thumb applies on the track as well. And now, with roller derby clothing outlets opening left, right and centre, all styles, colours and patterns of shorts, hotpants, leggings and skirts can be found. These can even be personalized with bespoke skate names added to the backs of tops, tunics or dresses, or even fighting-talk phrases to warn off opponents displayed on the back of a pair of booty shorts. Knee-high or over-the-knee socks are often worn, in team colours or with funky patterns such as stripes, or motifs such as skulls, polka dots or animal prints. Tights in a multitude of colours and patterns are available, and while some skaters choose to stick to a traditional fishnet, many ladies have been seen sporting lace, leopard, striped or multicoloured tights, or even stockings.

Kamikaze Kitten of the Ultraviolent Femmes, London Rollergirls, UK. Photo by Neal 'Hassle Brad' Humphris.

The Imposters Rollergirls, UK. Uniform t-shirt. Photo by Jason Ruffell.

Green and Blacks: The Fantastic Fourteen, Berlin Bombshells, Germany. Photo by Nadine Windberg.

Ferocious felines: the London Rockin' Rollers' Neanderdolls in leopard-print uniforms. Photo by Ray Lowe Studios.

US league Atlanta Rollergirls' Sake Tuyas team photo in Japanese-themed uniforms. Photo by Timothy Moxley.

Northside Rollers, Melbourne, Australia. Photo by Hana Schlesinger.

President Garfield of
Croydon Roller Derby, UK,
in grey and purple uniform.
Photo by Danny Bourne.

Kit Kat Power wears London Rockin' Rollers' red uniform dress. Photo by Danny Bourne.

Red n Roll of the London Rockin' Rollers, UK. Photo by Danny Bourne.

Demi Gore in team colours, Atlanta Rollergirls All Stars: the Dirty South Derby Girls, USA. Photo by Timothy Moxley.

LOGOS

Every roller derby league has its own distinctive logo, as do the different teams within each league. Many league logos tend to emphasize the location of the league using motifs and images associated with that particular city or area. The Gotham Girls Roller Derby from New York City, for example, use a motif based on the Statue of Liberty against the distinctive background of the New York skyline. The London Rollergirls' logo design, based on the distinctively British Union Jack flag, is another example of a location-based logo design, though this design is based on a national symbol, as this was the first roller derby league to be established in the UK.

However, league logos often subvert these distinctive regional or national motifs or images, often using different colours and distorting the traditional image to give it a unique anti-establishment edge. In the Gotham Girls Roller Derby logo, the New York skyline is set against a vivid background of red while the Statue of Liberty bears a feisty-looking grin complete with bright red lips and holds her hands in two tight fists, one adorned with a knuckle ring, braced and ready for a fight. The London Rollergirls' logo displays the Union Jack flag but, instead of the traditional red, white and blue, the colour scheme is tough but feminine pink and black, with the logo being pierced straight through the middle with a punk-style safety pin. The logo's text, 'London Rollergirls', has the effect of an arrangement of individual letters that have been cut out and pasted on, mimicking the text used in the album cover art of that quintessentially British punk band, The Sex Pistols.

The Kokeshi Roller Dolls of Okinawa, Japan are another perfect example of the national or cultural influence on logo designs. Like all roller derby leagues, they represent the area where the league was established; however, all the individual teams in their league also have culturally-influenced logos of their own. Each of their team logos are based on the characteristics of an Okinawan or Japanese name or subject combined with the attitude of derby, resulting in a combination of strong feminine and local influence. Their team names are the Sake Bombers, Habu Hellions, and Shisa Slammers.

Sake is the most famous of Japanese spirits, a sake bomb is a beer cocktail, and a bomb, of course, is an explosive. Bombs are threatening and dangerous, just like the rollergirls on the team. The logo shows an acme bomb ponytail bob and subliminal graphics portraying an 'X marks the spot' crosshair bullseye. The team's colours are dark green and yellow, representing the famous green bottles of *daiginjo*, one of the best types of sake.

A *habu* is an indigenous venomous pit viper found in the Ryukyu Islands. These nocturnal creatures can be found in dark caves between rocks. A hellion is a disorderly, troublesome, rowdy, or mischievous person. *Habu* and hellion make a perfect match to represent this team, who also like to strike quickly, are active at night and have a fiery attitude. The logo shows flaming red hair, a *habu* snake on the helmet, and distressed lettering as if it was so hot it cracked like a dried desert plain. The team's colours are dark red and gold representing fire and hell.

A *shisa* is a guardian lion dog, a traditional symbol in Okinawa mythology. *Shisas* come in pairs and, traditionally, the male *shisa's* mouth is closed to keep away bad spirits, while the female's mouth remains open to share goodness. The interpretation of this design comes complete with an open mouth, fangs, ears and curly hair, all representative of a *shisa*. Slammer is the perfect alliteration to define the hard hits from the skaters on the team. The team's colours are aqua and silver, representing the blue tropical shimmering waters of Okinawa.

Team logos are not always based on a specific location, however; some are purely thematic. Frequently using images or colour schemes associated with team names, team logos can complete the look defined by a team uniform. The London Rollergirls are comprised of four teams: The Harbour Grudges, the Ultraviolent Femmes, the Steam Rollers and the Suffra Jets. These team logos are purely thematic. The Harbour Grudges' uniform, for example, is based on a nautical theme with players skating in gold and navy blue. Their logo is comprised of a navy and white nautical star, finished with a gold anchor set in the centre of the star, which completes the look. The Steam Rollers have a steam-punk logo to go with their uniform, featuring a Victorian machine-style flying roller skate. The Suffra Jets' logo represents the feisty females of the future, set in space-age type in bright blue and purple hues. The Ultraviolent Femmes complete their Clockwork Orange theme with an image of a female ultraviolent brandishing a spanner, their team name underneath in a font straight out of Kubrick's legendary film.

Kokeshi Roller Dolls, Japan. League logo. Designed by John Fitzpatrick and Pisa Cake.

London Rollergirls, UK.
League logo.

Ultraviolent Femmes team
logo, London Rollergirls, UK.

Steam Rollers' team logo,
London Rollergirls, UK.

Harbour Grudges logo,
London Rollergirls, UK.

Gotham Girls Roller
Derby logo, USA.

Suffra Jets' team logo, London
Rollergirls, UK.

Hula Gunn of London Rollergirls, UK wearing Ultraviolent Femmes uniform. Photo by Neal 'Hassle Brad' Humphris.

Derby Stopout of the London Rockin' Rollers wears black uniform T-shirt and ladies Y-fronts with logo designed by Vince Ray. Photo by Danny Bourne.

NAMES, CHARACTERS AND PERSONAL STYLES

Roller derby is a sport with room for all styles and personalities – the bigger and quirkier, the better. It's a sport that attracts people with a strong sense of individuality, a characteristic that is undoubtedly celebrated in roller derby culture.

Hyper Nova, Stockholm Roller Derby, Sweden. Photo by Sleaze Machine.

From the very beginning of the sport, big personalities have always been popular among skaters and spectators alike. In the original Transcontinental Roller Derby of the 1930s Josephine 'Ma' Bogash was one of Leo Seltzer's first notorious femmes fatales – she drew in crowds to match her big personality and dangerous antics on the track. 'Ma' got her nickname because she was famed for skating in a pair with her son Billy. She was rumoured to carry a hatpin in her hair to enable her to move ruthlessly through the pack.

In the original roller derbies, skater rivalries were very popular among fans. Gerry Murray and Toughie Brasuhn were one of the first examples of such rivalries. Gerry Murray was a pretty, all-American darling, while Toughie was rough and ready, and their battles on the track enthralled the audiences of the day.

The roller derby of the 1950s and '60s was littered with big personalities who became household names among their many fans. Players such as Joan Weston and Ann Calvello are revered today as

> **Ann Calvello joined the roller derby in 1948 and played professionally for a total of seven decades, even appearing as honorary guest at a bout in 2005. She was known by fans as the 'demon of derby', 'banana nose' and the 'meanest mama on skates'.**

the original 'personalities' of roller derby. They are the great heroes of many a skater in the current revival. Ann Calvello joined the roller derby in 1948 and played professionally for a total of seven decades, even appearing as honorary guest at a bout in 2005. She was known by fans as the 'demon of derby', 'banana nose' and the 'meanest mama on skates'. Famed for her sass, her 'bad girl' attitude and living dangerously on the track, Ann Calvello was distinguished by her tattoos, her multicoloured hair, her deep tan, her pre-dated punk-rock attitude, and for spending lengthy periods in the penalty box. She was known for her outstanding endurance and athletic ability, withstanding many injuries during her time on the track. Twelve broken noses, four broken elbows, a broken collarbone, a broken tailbone and blindness in one eye didn't stop her from playing her beloved sport. It was a sad day for the roller derby community when she died of liver cancer in 2006 and she will always be remembered.

With the establishment of the San Francisco Bay Bombers in 1958 came the historic rivalry between Ann Calvello and Joan Weston. Joan

Ann Calvello, the 'demon of derby'. Photo provided by Getty.

Superhero style: Vesper Synd, London Rollergirls Recreational League, UK. Photo by Danny Bourne.

Kamikatze completes her cat girl persona with tattoo and matching face mask, Fantastic Fourteen, Berlin Bombshells, Germany. Photo by Nadine Windberg.

Poison Ivy of the Fantastic Fourteen, Berlin Bombshells, Germany. Photo by Nadine Windberg.

Western belles: The Good, The Bad and The Gorgeous, Berlin Bombshells, Germany style it up. Photo by Miss Van D.

Weston was Calvello's famous on-track rival, creating a tension in the game that sent the crowds wild. She was the antithesis of Calvello, the 'good girl' in contrast to the mad, bad and dangerous 'demon of derby'. Also known as the 'blonde bomber', Weston was famed for her golden girl looks, her athletic physique and her strong but fair gameplay.

From the lightning speed of the Gotham Girls' Suzy Hotrod, her muscular arms adorned with their signature tattoos, to the leaps and bounds of Steel City's Hurricane Heather, her long dreadlocks flailing in the wind as she flies around the track, today there are just as many big on-track personalities and skate styles as there were back in the day.

With the characters of today's roller derby revival came the advent of the 'derby name' or pseudonym by which the majority of skaters are known on the track. Since the formation of Bad Girl Good Woman Productions in Texas, it has become tradition that most skaters adopt a unique nom de guerre to skate under.

These skate names are often great feats of wordplay and pun-craft, with a healthy dose of humour added to the mix. Names are often based on allusions to well-known figures in film, music or other parts of popular culture – for example, Gotham Girls' Beyonslay, Rita Hateworth of the Atlanta Rollergirls or Audrey Rugburn of the Denver Roller Dolls.

Racey Slam Hard of London Rollergirls, UK, wears custom top by Wicked Skatewear. Photo by Danny Bourne.

Kim Oh No of Sheffield Steel Rollergirls, UK. Photo by Jason Ruffell.

WhipIt wears London Rockin' Rollers' red uniform T-shirt and ladies' Y-fronts. Photo by Danny Bourne.

Puns on well-known phrases such as London Rollergirls' Grievous Bodily Charm, Vigour Mortis and Vital Sadistic are often adapted to create a mock-violent edge. Single words associated with violence are also adapted to become names such as Anna Mosity of the Jet City Rollergirls.

Derby names have to be unique for both practical and personal reasons, as not only would the skaters dislike having the same name, but in a bout situation it would be impossible for the referees to distinguish between two identically named opponents. Every skater must register their name on a master roster online at www.twoevils.org/ rollergirls, and new skaters are required to check the roster to ensure that there isn't another player skating under the name they've chosen. Those with names similar to an existing name have to be granted permission by the original player with that name to use an adaptation of it. Names starting with possessives or ending with a gerund are not allowed, as this would also be too confusing for the referees. The appropriation of a derby name is often seen as a badge of honour as, in most leagues, a

Puns on well-known phrases such as London Rollergirls' Grievous Bodily Charm, Vigour Mortis and Vital Sadistic are often adapted to create a mock-violent edge.

minimum training period, commitment and skill level are required before a skater is able to register their name.

Skate names are often related to a skater's personality or interests off the track. For example, Hydra, former skater from Texas Rollergirls, previous president and one of the founders of WFTDA, chose her skate name because she is a hydrologist by profession and had taken a class in Greek mythology when she started skating. After discovering that Hydra, the mythological water beast was an indestructible creature with nine heads, she decided to appropriate this name to ensure she was indestructible on the track.

Some skaters use the opportunity of adopting a pseudonym to create their own heroic 'alter ego' or 'persona'. These often come in the form of plays on the names of strong heroines from popular culture, caricatures of superheroes (or heroines), pin-ups and other powerful stereotypes. Not all rollergirls are as naturally 'mean' or 'feisty' as they are assumed to be – some are actually quite shy. Many skaters claim that assuming an 'alter ego' on the track helps them to become the powerful and

Helen Nash of London Rollergirls, UK skates under her real name. Photo provided by Getty.

The Bexorcist and Sugar Bump of London Rollergirls, UK. Photo provided by Getty.

fearsome player they want to be, as they are liberated from what their natural reaction might be or what people who know them personally would expect them to do in certain situations. Teammates are often the best of friends but when they are playing roller derby, they have to be prepared to go in for full-contact hits with no reservations.

Taking on a derby persona can also provide an excuse for skaters to wear fabulous, daring and outrageous clothes that they would never wear outside of derby. Corresponding fashion styles are often constructed to complement a skater's derby name and also their 'persona'. This can be anything from simple warpaint to an entirely themed boutfit. The Atlanta Rollergirls team the Sake Tuyas includes Edna Vendetta, the Japanese street-style ninja with geisha-inspired make-up and a rotating blade on standby, and Polly Atomic, the mad scientist who has escaped the lab wearing not much more than her lab coat, roller skates and derby uniform. Stockholm Roller Derby is also home to Girl Interrupted, fresh from the asylum and still wearing her straightjacket, and Toxic Waist, complete with gas mask and high-risk black-and-yellow-striped hazard tape.

However, not all rollergirls buy into the notion of adopting a persona or alter ego on the track. Over the last few years, a contrary movement of players skating under their real names has begun. A group of skaters

from a variety of different leagues in the US who wanted to skate under their real names formed Team Legit, and now skate under their ordinary names in tournaments in different parts of the country. Skaters in other leagues have since followed suit, with two of the London Rollergirls, Stephanie Mainey, once known as Correctional Felicity, and Helen Nash, once known as Viva Kneivil, having ditched their pseudonyms in recent years. The use of real names is preferred by some skaters because they believe that using a skate name detracts from the athleticism of roller derby and that the sport will be taken more seriously if real names are used. Helen Nash acknowledges this in an interview in UK derby 'zine *Rollerama*, stating that 'The athleticism and strategic gameplay I admire far outshines any flashy outfit or pun-tastic name.' This is understandable, as the use of personas or alter egos appeals more to the performance aspect of roller derby than its athleticism.

Blood on the flat track. Skater from Northside Rollers Melbourne, Australia. Photo by Hana Schlesinger.

Rollin out the high fashion. Northside Rollers, Melbourne, Australia. Photo by Hana Schlesinger.

Nickel Nutz of the Shisa Slammers, Kokeshi Roller Dolls, Japan. Photo by Christopher A. Baldwin.

Polly Atomic of the Sake Tuyas, Atlanta Rollergirls, USA. Photo by Timothy Moxley.

Milky Madness, Stockholm Roller Derby, Sweden. Photo by Sleaze Machine.

Sexy ninja Edna Vendetta of the Sake Tuyas, Atlanta Rollergirls, USA. Photo by Timothy Moxley.

Billie the Anger of The Good, The Bad and The Gorgeous, Berlin Bombshells, Germany. Photo by Miss Van D.

Girl Interrupted, Stockholm Roller Derby, Sweden. Photo by Sleaze Machine.

Toxic Waist, Stockholm Roller Derby, Sweden. Photo by Sleaze Machine.

ESSENTIAL KIT AND SKATES

Roller derby is a fast and dangerous sport, so every player must be prepared to be knocked down and hit hard at high speed. There are certain items necessary to play the sport, providing players with protection from potential injuries. In any given bout, no player is allowed to play in the game unless they are wearing the following essential items, and for the players' safety all kit is checked by the referees to ensure it is fitted correctly.

Derby skates. Ladies of Hell Town, Sao Paolo, Brazil. Photo by Antonio Soares.

ESSENTIAL KIT

KNEE PADS
ELBOW PADS
WRIST GUARDS
MOUTH GUARD
HELMET

KNEE PADS

These are among the most important items of kit you can buy. Roller derby is extremely hard on the knees, especially for those players who get knocked down a lot, so maximum knee protection is essential. There are several brands of knee pads favoured by roller derby players that cater specifically to their needs. Smith Scabs knee pads are one brand favoured by rollergirls around the world. These large pads provide maximum protection for the knee and are designed to stay in place. They even come in limited-edition fabrics such as leopard print or the psychedelic-patterned Hypno pad. Other brands of knee pads favoured by roller derby skaters are 187 Killer Pads, TSG, Triple 8 and Protec, among others, most of which are also used for other extreme

sports such as skateboarding and snowboarding. There are even pads available custom-made in a skater's colours or patterns of choice to match team or league uniforms, or as part of a unique look that expresses the individual skater's personal taste.

ELBOW PADS AND WRIST GUARDS

These are also essential, though when you're playing roller derby your elbows and wrists don't take quite as much of a battering as your knees. Skaters often favour the same makers of wrist and elbow pads as those that make knee pads, and as with those items custom colours, patterns and fabrics are also an option. There are subtle differences between brands, but really it comes down to personal preference.

MOUTH GUARD

This is another very important part of the kit bag. No one wants to lose their teeth or bite through their lip in the middle of a jam, so a good strong mouth guard that fits properly is a must-have. Of course, the whole concept of a mouth guard seems unnatural. After all, who wants to hold a large piece of plastic in their mouth for long periods of time? However, there are now plenty of mouth guards, specially designed for roller derby, which can be moulded to ensure maximum comfort and a

President Garfield of Croydon Roller Derby, UK, wearing mouthguard. Photo by Danny Bourne.

Smiths Scabs knee pads in leopard, black and Hypno fabrics. Photo by Danny Bourne.

Mackenzie Knepp from the Red Ridin' Hoods of Rocky Mountain Rollergirls, USA, lines up to jam. Photo by Amanda Renee, Wicked Shamrock Photography.

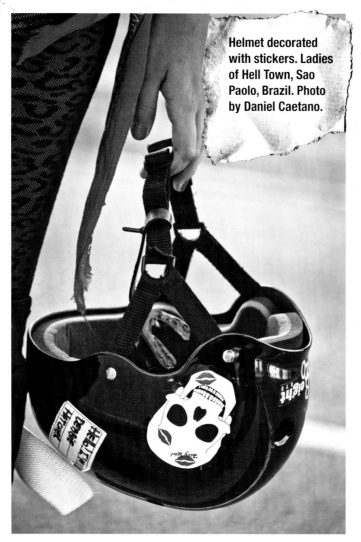

Helmet decorated with stickers. Ladies of Hell Town, Sao Paolo, Brazil. Photo by Daniel Caetano.

Protection in style: Erin No Bragh of London Rollergirls, UK, wears fang mouthgard. Photo by Danny Bourne.

perfect fit. Mouth guards for roller derby are designed by the fashion-conscious and can be found in a range of colours, or featuring designs such as vampire fangs, or printed with custom phrases or skate names such as Sinister or D. Stroir.

HELMET

In some ways, the helmet is the most important part of a skater's kit. Though hits to the head are illegal and hitting your head on the floor only happens as a result of a particularly nasty hit or fall, the head needs maximum protection at all times. Skaters often customize their helmets with skate names or other personal designs, or by collaging stickers with slogans, skate-wear brand names and other roller derby team and league names and logos collected from bouts or tournaments.

OTHER KIT

There are many other bits of kit used in addition to these essentials, to aid performance and to provide additional protection on the track. These are:

Knee gaskets

Shin guards and ankle supports
Padded shorts
Lower back, spine and chest protection
Toecaps for skates
Tape

KNEE GASKETS

These can also be worn underneath knee pads to increase protection. Knee gaskets are used in order to provide:

- additional impact protection
- kneecap stabilization
- an under layer that helps hard shell knee pads stay in place
- warmth around the knee area

SHIN GUARDS AND ANKLE SUPPORTS

Roller derby skaters often experience injuries, so sometimes added protection is a necessity. Ankles, knees and shins are particularly vulnerable, and additional pads are available on top of the essential kit, to provide further protection to these areas.

Mentally Un-Mayble of London Rollergirls Recreational League wearing roller derby gear by Wicked Skatewear and Pivotstar and Smiths Scabs 'Hypno' knee pads. Photo by Danny Bourne.

PADDED SHORTS

Nothing hurts quite like falling on your arse at high speed, and this is something that happens very frequently in roller derby. Padded shorts, some with added tailbone protection, are worn by certain players to protect themselves against nasty falls.

LOWER BACK, SPINE AND CHEST PROTECTION

For players who have suffered back injuries, extra padding and 'body armour' are also available to protect areas such as the spine and lower back from injury. Though the back is an illegal zone for hitting in roller derby, accidents can still happen. The chest, however, is a legal hitting zone, and chest protection is available for rollergirls who want to protect their assets, or 'tickets' as Ann Calvello famously referred to them.

TOECAPS

Derby skates are prone to getting a good battering, so many skaters choose to protect the leather uppers of the toes of their skates using a cover. These now come in a range of colours and materials, making this another way to style up your skates. However, some people prefer just to tape them up.

TAPE

Gaffer tape is often used in bout situations to tape pads onto the body, to ensure that pad straps hold pads firmly in place and don't get caught on other skaters.

Derby skates. Ladies of Hell Town, Sao Paolo, Brazil. Photo by Daniel Caetano.

The Atlanta Rollergirls All Stars The Dirty South Derby Girls go barefoot. Photo by Timothy Moxley.

Kim Oh No wears bespoke skate-name necklace, Sheffield Steel Rollergirls, UK. Photo by Jason Ruffell.

Sin D. Doll of London Rockin' Rollers, UK and Jeopardy Jinx of Croydon Roller Derby on the jammer line. Photo by Danny Bourne.

SKATES

HISTORY OF THE ROLLER SKATE

It has taken centuries to perfect the design of the roller skates that we know and love today. The roller skate has been through many different evolutionary stages over some three centuries up to the current design, and is constantly being innovated to this day.

The first-ever roller skates were invented in 1760 in London, England by John Joseph Merlin. These were in-line skates and were very difficult to manoeuvre. Merlin was a well-known inventor and decided to debut his new invention by wearing the skates to a party, where he famously crashed into a large mirror. Some say this fiasco was the reason the skates were not seen again for almost 60 years, as they were thought to be very dangerous.

The next incarnation appeared in 1819 in Paris, France, courtesy of a Monsieur Petitbled, who was the first person known to have patented the invention of the roller skate. Petitbled's skates were also in-line, with three wheels made of wood, metal or ivory. They had wooden soles and leather straps to hold them in place. However, these skates could only move forwards, and stopping and turning corners proved very difficult. The design was yet to be perfected for general use.

In 1863 the American James Leonard Plimpton patented a new type of roller skate that would change the sport forever. Having been frustrated by the limitations of the previous in-line-style skates, Plimpton invented a four-wheel roller skate, also known as the 'rocking skate', that was capable of turning. The mechanism had a pivoting action dampened by a rubber cushion which permitted the roller skater to curve by leaning in the direction they wanted to travel, much like the roller skates used today.

Plimpton built a public roller skating space in the office of his furniture business in New York where people could hire his skates. He later founded the New York Roller Skating Association (NYRSA). The NYRSA opened the first public roller skating rink in 1866 at the Atlantic House resort hotel in Rhode Island. Plimpton is credited with the establishment of roller skating as a popular sport.

Other improvements to the roller skate design were made in subsequent decades, the first of which was William Brown's 1876 patented design for an improvement to the wheels of roller skates, which kept the two bearing surfaces of an axle, fixed and moving, apart. The first toe-stop for roller skates was also patented in 1876, and the following year Joseph Henry Hughes worked closely with Brown to patent the ball- or roller-bearing race for bicycle and carriage wheels. Together, Brown and Hughes were responsible for revolutionizing roller skate and skateboard wheels, as well as the wheels of bicycles and velocipedes, which were later to become automobiles and motorbikes.

In 1884 Levant M. Richardson patented the use of steel ball bearings, which, by reducing friction in the wheels of roller skates, allowed skaters to increase their speed with minimum effort. By the late 1880s roller skates were being mass-produced in the US by Micajah C. Henley. Henley was also responsible for the development of the first kingpin-style mechanism, giving the skate adjustable tension by means of a screw. The design of the quad skate has remained almost unchanged since then, bar a few small changes, such as the introduction of plastic wheels during the 1970s.

During the early 20th century, roller skating evolved from a pastime into a variety of different sports including roller hockey, speed skating, figure skating, jam skating and, of course, roller derby. The Roller Skating Rink Operators' Association was established in the US in 1937 and is still operating today as the Roller Skating Association. Roller skating continued to grow in popularity throughout the 1940s, '50s and '60s.

There are now many different varieties of roller skates, all specifically designed for different skating purposes, roller derby being only one of them. A lot of people begin roller skating in a roller disco situation, where artistic roller skates are available for hire. Artistic skates are

Petitbled Skate, 1819. Photo provided by the National Roller Skating Museum, Nebraska, USA.

Plimpton Skate, 1863. Photo provided by the National Roller Skating Museum, Nebraska, USA.

designed for skating in a traditional roller disco or roller rink and are usually high-cut boots with a toe stop at the front. The high-cut boot design gives the skater more control when doing jumps or spins. This type of roller skate boot often has a higher heel so that the skater's weight is distributed more onto the toes, allowing the manoeuvrability required for dance moves. Different types of specially designed skates are available for speed skating, usually featuring a low-cut boot that sits just below the anklebone. The heels of the boot are usually very low, and larger wheels with added potential for speed are often used.

Jam skating combines dance, gymnastics and skating in dance-style moves or routines performed on roller skates. Jam skaters originally wore traditional artistic skates, but in the early 1980s a new trend developed for wearing low-cut speed-skate boots with dance plugs instead of toe stops. These skates, which continue to be popular to this day, are preferred by some jam skaters as the low-cut boot allows for more agility while skating.

Other types of quad skates include hockey quad skates for roller hockey. These are often made from hockey boots mounted on a quad plate. Aggressive quad skates usually feature a wider truck for greater stability when landing jumps, and a grinding plate as seen on aggressive in-line skates. Grinding plates are fitted on the bottom of the skate for sliding along curbs and rails. All-terrain or mountain skates are made with very large tractor-style wheels and wide trucks to withstand all terrains and surfaces.

Roller derby skates have a low-cut boot and a low heel, much like speed skates. The front axle is often located right under the ball of the foot for more manoeuvrability. A wide variety of wheels is available for different skaters' preferences and track surfaces.

London Rockin' Rollers accessorize with different tights, socks, skates and pads. Photo by Danny Bourne.

THE ANATOMY OF THE SKATE

A roller derby skate is made up of the following different parts:

Boot
Plates
Kingpins
Trucks
Axles
Axle nut
Pivot points
Pivot cup
Bushings (cushions)
Toe stops
Toe-stop nut and washer
Wheels
Bearings

ADDITIONAL KIT FOR SKATES

Skate accessories such as brightly coloured or glittery laces
Skate tool for adjusting skates, changing wheels and skate maintenance
Grease for bearings

Boot

The skate boot is the upper, shoe-like part of the skate. This is often made of leather, though vegan skates are also available.

Plates

The plate is attached to the skate boot with nuts and bolts. The plate supports the wheels and toe stops and forms the pivot points, enabling the skate to turn. Plates can be made of different materials but all function in the same way. Cheaper plates are usually made from plastic or nylon, with better-quality plates being made from aluminium. The highest quality plates are usually made from tempered aircraft-grade aluminium. This material is both very strong and lightweight, enabling the skater to skate faster and harder, and to jump higher without risk of breaking the skates.

Kingpins

Each plate has kingpins attached to it, one at the front and one at the back, which support the wheel assemblies. The front one is tilted a little towards the front, while the back one tilts towards the back. The angle of the kingpin helps the skate to steer when pressure is applied to one side of the skate or the other.

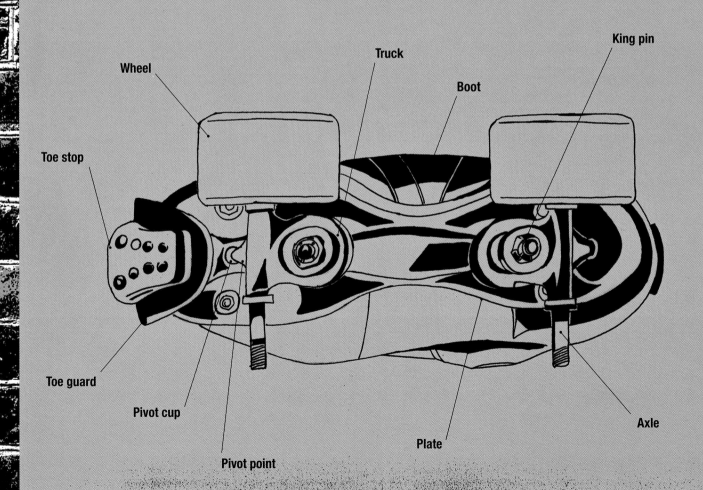

Trucks

The skate trucks are fitted onto each kingpin, one at the front and one at the back. Each truck is mounted between two rubber bushings, which are also fitted to the kingpins. The trucks also have pivot points attached to them which fit into a slot on the base of the plate.

Axles

The axles are metal pins that come off the trucks. These go through the middle of the bearings, attaching the wheels to the skate. The axle nut holds the wheels in place at the end of each axle.

Pivot points

The pivot points are attached to each truck and fit into a slot on the base of the plate called the pivot cup. The pivot points act as fixed points around which the axles can twist.

Bushings (cushions)

Each truck is mounted between two rubber bushings (also known as cushions) and held in place with a nut. The hardness of the bushings and the tightness of this nut controls the steering sensitivity of the roller skates. Harder bushings will make the turning action stiffer but do provide more stability for less confident skaters. However, softer bushings are recommended for roller derby skaters, as they make turning easier and the skate more responsive.

Toe stops

Toe stops screw into a threaded hole at the front of each plate. The length of the shaft of the toe stop can be adjusted. Some prefer a long shaft so that the stop is closer to the floor. Other skaters prefer a stop with a much shorter shaft, which may be easier to run on. Toe stops are very important in roller derby as they are used as a fast-track acceleration device by many skaters. It is much easier to run on your toe stops to pick up speed than to run on your wheels, which are moving. Artistic skaters use the toe stops in a similar way as the launch platform for many of their high-level jumps; jam skaters often don't use toe stops, but just plug the holes with what is called a 'jam plug'.

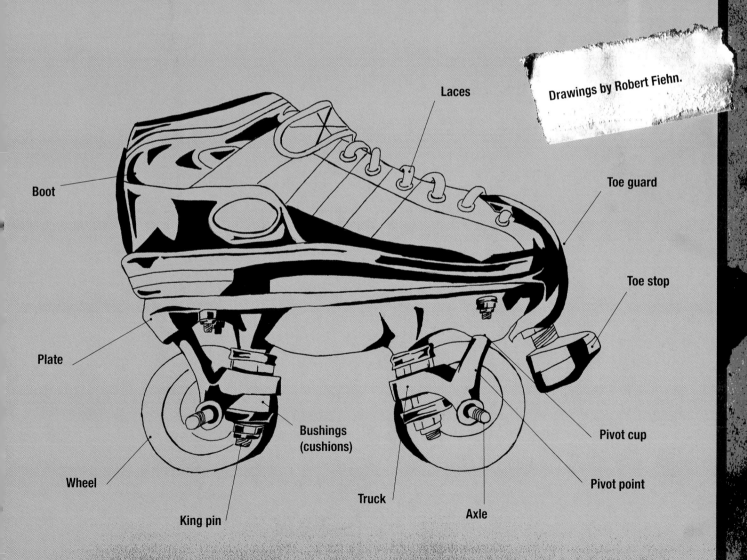

Drawings by Robert Fiehn.

Laces

Boot

Toe guard

Toe stop

Plate

Bushings (cushions)

Pivot cup

Wheel

Pivot point

Truck

King pin

Axle

Wheels

Wheels can be different sizes and made of different materials, each of which have different benefits. These are debated and discussed endlessly by derby skaters and referees alike. There are now many companies creating wheels specially designed for roller derby and the needs that every skater experiences. Whether it's a wider wheel with a lot of grip to ensure stability on a slippery floor, or slimmer wheels to increase agility within the pack, there are wheels designed for all purposes and personal preferences.

Roller-skate wheels are constructed from a hub, made of either metal or plastic, which supports the wheel bearings. A rubber tyre, usually made from urethane, is moulded onto the outside of the hub. Wheel tyres are given an 'A rating' which refers to their hardness – the higher the rating, the harder the tyre. These ratings range from 70A to 103A. Generally, wheels of 85A rating or above are used for skating indoors or on very smooth surfaces, while those below 85A are used for rough outdoor surfaces such as pavements. These softer wheels are better for skating outdoors as they can more easily absorb the uneven surfaces of roads or pavements, making them easier to skate on. The harder wheels used for indoor skating vary because indoor floor surfaces provide very different skating experiences and different wheels are required for skating on wood, lino and other types of floors. There are wheels designed specially for very slippery floors so that skaters have as much control as possible to avoid slipping. Some wheels have micro-grooves moulded into them to improve grip still further, while others are completely smooth. The width of a wheel also affects skating but is down to personal preference. A wider wheel will have more grip than a narrow one, because more of the rubber is in contact with the ground.

Atom Wheels 'Poisons', side view. Photo provided by Atom Wheels.

Bearings

Skate wheels turn freely because of an anti-friction device called a bearing inserted between each wheel and axle. Skate bearings reduce the friction between a moving skate wheel and a fixed, non-moving skate frame. Each wheel has two bearings located in the centre, which fit onto the roller skate's axles. Each pair of roller skates will have 16 wheel bearings in total. Bearings are made from a casing containing several balls which can be made of different materials depending on the bearing. They are often made of steel, though many skaters prefer ceramic bearings, which are lighter, smoother, harder and corrosion-resistant. Full ceramic bearings with ceramic casing as well as ceramic balls are also available but are often very expensive.

Bearings are usually rated on a scale defined by the Annular Bearing Engineers' Committee, or ABEC. This is known as the ABEC rating, and will be either 1, 3, 5, 7 or 9. The number relates to tolerances used in its manufacture, with 1 being the lowest rating and 9 the highest. It is commonly thought that higher-rated bearings allow you to skate faster. However, the speed the bearing runs at is determined primarily by the lubricant used inside the bearing. A bearing lubricated with thick grease will generally run slower than one lubricated with light oil. An ABEC 9 bearing will run smoother and quieter than an ABEC 1 bearing, and will last longer, but generally it will not affect the speed at which they roll.

When buying bearings, it is important to buy the right size bearings for your axles. Most trucks made in the US have 8mm diameter axles, whereas European manufacturers tend to prefer 7mm axles. The right size bearings are essential or they won't fit.

Atom Wheels 'Pulse', side view. Photo provided by Atom Wheels.

Bones Reds bearings. Photo provided by Bones Bearings.

Riedell skates with Radar Tile Biter wheels in orange. Photo by Danny Bourne.

Skates worn by The Imposters Rollergirls, UK. Photo by Jason Ruffell.

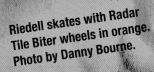

Miss Trouble fixes Na'Dynamite's skates, both of the Psycho Rollers, Buenos Aires Roller Derby, Argentina. Photo by Nestor Benitez.

Skaters from London Rollergirls Recreational League wearing a range of skates and pads. Photo by Danny Bourne.

REFEREES, NSOS AND MALE ROLLER DERBY

Since 2001, roller derby has been a female-dominated sport. However, men have always been involved in the roller derby revival, often in supporting roles such as referees or other non-skating officials as these roles can be taken on by males or females even if the league they belong to is a women's league. Roller derby is now becoming increasingly popular among men with male leagues and teams forming at a rapid rate. Both male and female referees and non-skating officials, as well as male derby skaters have their very own fashion and individual styles as they are just as much a part of the show as the female skaters.

Blow Up Doll, referee from Castle Rock N Rollers, USA, wearing pink frilly hotpants. Photo by Amanda Renee, Wicked Shamrock Photography.

REFEREES

The referees' job in roller derby is the same as in other sports: to make sure everyone remains safe and plays by the rules. The rules of roller derby are very long and complex with many different nuances for different situations. The game is often played so fast that it is difficult for the skaters to know whether they have committed an offence, even if they are very familiar with the rules. There may be disputes, strops and even tears, but the referees' word is always final.

In order to ensure the safety of the skaters, the referees have several duties to fulfil, the first of which is to make sure all skaters are fully protected with all the essential safety equipment; that this equipment is in good condition; and that it fits correctly. At the beginning of any bout, all the skaters in both teams line up to have their equipment checked by the referees. If the referees find a skater is missing any part of their kit, or that it doesn't fit, then they will not be able to compete in the bout. Their other duties include counting points scored by each jammer; keeping track of the timings for each jam and the overall game clocks; communicating with the announcers, scorekeepers and team captains; calling out penalties; and stopping the game in case of injury.

> **There may be disputes, strops and even tears, but the referees' word is always final.**

In a bout or any scrimmage situation, referees will call players for committing major or minor penalties during the game. The breaking of some rules means an immediate 'major' penalty is given, but in some situations a 'minor' is given depending on the severity of the foul committed and the effect it has on other skaters. A major penalty results in the offending skater being sent to the penalty box, where they must stay for a total of one minute after which they can re-enter the pack behind all the other skaters playing in that jam. If a skater receives a major penalty, they are immediately sent off. Four minor penalties also result in a major and the player being sent off. Five major penalties result in the player being ejected from the game.

With multiple players making full contact at any given time, it would be impossible for one referee to be able to keep an eye on all the skaters at the same time. Thus there are several different types of referee in roller derby, because in this fast-paced sport there are too many jobs for one referee to do alone. Indeed, there can be up to seven referees on duty in a given bout.

Camp David, referee for London Rollergirls, UK. Photo provided by Getty.

Zebras get creative: Blow Up Doll, referee for Castle Rock N Rollers, USA. Photo by Amanda Renee, Wicked Shamrock Photography.

Referee Cruel Hand Luke. Photo by Amanda Renee, Wicked Shamrock Photography.

DIFFERENT TYPES OF REFEREES

Jammer referees

In a roller derby bout, there is always one referee watching each jammer closely. They watch from the inside of the track and signify who is the lead jammer, i.e. the jammer that breaks through the pack first. The jammer referees count the number of points their jammer is scoring. They must keep a close eye on any major or minor penalties committed by their jammer and ultimately keep the players safe.

Pack referees

The pack referees watch from both the inside and outside of the track. Their job is to keep an eye on the main pack skaters, watching out for any penalties. There are usually four pack referees watching the jam at all times to enforce any necessary penalties for infringements of the rules.

Head referee

The head referee has the last word on all situations and the final say in disputes. He or she instructs the other referees on who is to do what in the game.

REFEREES' UNIFORMS

Roller derby referees are known as 'zebras' because of their black and white uniforms. Although the referees are all required to wear the standard black and white vertical-striped outfits, many individual interpretations of this get-up are seen on the track. Referees can be either men or women, and it tends to be the women who make creative adaptations to their uniforms, sporting skirts and dresses of many different styles and variations by recycling the traditional zebra-striped shirt.

Zebras get creative: Blow Up Doll, referee for Castle Rock N Rollers, USA. Photo by Amanda Renee, Wicked Shamrock Photography.

Referees and Non Skating Officials (NSOs) also have derby names in the same way that the skaters do. These are composed using the same principles of wit and showmanship and are displayed on the back of uniforms.

NSOS

In addition to the referees, there are also at least six NSOs or non-skating officials. The NSOs help referees to co-ordinate the game, and they too have a variety of different jobs to do off the track. The NSOs include scorekeepers who are informed by the jammer referees of the number of points scored in each jam, and keep track of the total scores throughout the game. They share this information with the scoreboard operator, who communicates it to the audience on either a digital or a manual scoreboard, depending on the venue.

The NSOs are also in charge of the penalty box. They include penalty timers whose job it is to time skaters in the penalty box to make sure they serve the correct amount of time. The penalty trackers are

responsible for keeping count of how many penalties each player has been given.

OTHER SUPPORTING CREW

There is a whole host of other supporting crew involved in roller derby leagues without which bout situations would be a lot less entertaining.

Announcers provide live commentary for the audiences at games; there is half-time entertainment in the form of DJs, bands, dancers or cheerleaders; then there are the coaches; and, of course, the all-important fans complete the picture of roller derby today.

It tends to be the women who make creative adaptations to their uniforms, sporting skirts and dresses of many different styles and variations by recycling the traditional zebra-striped shirt.

Atlanta Rollergirls' referees. Photo by Timothy Moxley.

Rage Appropriate, Atlanta Rollergirls' referee, USA. Photo by Timothy Moxley.

MEN'S ROLLER DERBY OR 'MERBY'

Men's roller derby, or 'merby' as it is now known, began in 2006 with the launch of Pioneer Valley Roller Derby in Northampton, Massachusetts. When Sarah Lang, aka Pink Panza, and her boyfriend Jake Fahy, aka Bazooka Joe, started up the league, they decided to establish teams for both men and women. The first men's team was called the Dirty Dozen. Their first scrimmage in public was organized by Justice Feelgood Marshall, a referee for Charm City Roller Girls, and it took place at half-time during the Charm City bout. Justice Feelgood Marshall went on to form Harm City Homicide in 2007 and from then on more men's leagues were established, led by the New York Shock Exchange and the Death Quads of Connecticut.

In 2007 these leagues formed the Men's Derby Coalition, now known as the Men's Roller Derby Association, to create a community for

male derby skaters and to share resources and knowledge they have gained through their collective experiences. On their website, the MRDA promise 'to foster the development of sustainable roller derby leagues, to cultivate positive sportsmanship on and off the track, and to enhance the derby community' as well as providing 'new leagues with direction and encouragement while offering strategic benefits to member leagues'.

As with WFTDA, all the member leagues in the MRDA are skater-owned and -operated and have a say in the development of the organization's policies. The MRDA maintains standards for rules, safety and gameplay for local, regional and international competitions. With the support of WFTDA, the MRDA aims to build a similarly influential brother organization for men's roller derby leagues.

There are now 18 men's leagues in the MRDA and new men's teams and leagues are forming all the time. Men's leagues in the US, UK and Australia have multiplied in recent years, with men's roller derby become increasingly international as the sport grows in general.

> There are now 18 men's leagues in the MRDA and new men's teams and leagues are forming all the time.

The Dirty Dozen, Pioneer Valley Roller Derby, USA in military-style uniforms. Photo by Asa Frye.

The Dirty Dozen, Pioneer Valley Roller Derby, USA in military-style uniforms. Photo by Asa Frye.

Men's teams and leagues place a lot less emphasis on roller derby fashion in general, with most skaters wearing functional sportswear or skate wear. However, most male teams have a uniform and a logo in the same way as female teams. A lot of men's team uniforms have a pronounced masculine look – for example, Pioneer Valley's Dirty Dozen have a distinctly military theme to their uniform. Most male skaters wear a uniform t-shirt with sports or combat shorts, in a similar style to skateboarders or aggressive in-line skaters. In some leagues, where there are men's and women's teams, uniforms are co-ordinated so that the men's boutfits resemble the women's.

Some men play on the fact that they are a minority in this female-dominated sport and have been known to play in skirts as a humorous twist. Male derby skaters can often be seen wearing make up or war paint at bouts, much like their female equivalents and sporting humorous masculine skate names.

War paint: not just for girls. Twisted Mister of Central City Rollergirls, UK, men's team. Photo by Jason Ruffell.

Average Joes vs Rocky Mountain Riot, USA. Photo by Amanda Renee, Wicked Shamrock Photography.

98

New York Shock Exchange, USA men's roller derby league in black and white uniforms. Photo by Asa Frye.

Jammie Dodger jamming for Tyne and Fear men's roller derby team, UK. Photo by Jason Ruffell.

Connecticut Death Quads' uniform T-shirt. Photo by Asa Frye.

London Rockin' Rollers' bench coach Smirkcules in red hotpants. Photo by Danny Bourne.

Chemic Al of Tyne and Fear men's roller derby team, UK, wearing team uniform. Photo by Jason Ruffell.

HAIR, MAKE-UP AND TATTOOS

Roller derby skaters can adorn themselves and express their personal style with more than just clothes and skates – tattoos in a multitude of styles are often on display, as well as facial and body piercings and creative hairstyles often in different colours.

Perhaps because the roller derby revival of the last ten years has developed under a skater-owned DIY aesthetic, a lot of roller derby players are creative and stylish people who find diverse and interesting ways to express themselves.

'This ass was made for blocking': Brat O'Tat and Rakel Riot of Red Stick Roller Derby, USA. Photo by Akoch Photography, LLC. © 2011

HAIR

All types of hairstyles can be found in roller derby. From long, flowing girly locks to razor-blade short crops or dreadlocks in a variety of colours, to trendy ironic mullets and undercut or partially shaved styles. Short haircuts and pin-up girl styles with short blunt fringes are often popular, as are bleached tresses and multicoloured coiffures. Even back in the heyday of the 1950s, the ladies used to get creative with their bouffants to create their signature look: Joanie Weston was famously known as the 'golden girl' of roller derby because of her healthy glow and blond mop of hair. Ann Calvello used to get creative with her hair, often sporting multicoloured looks years before the punk look was born.

Helmet hair is often a big problem for roller girls. What's a girl to do when she finishes up on the track and whips off her helmet to find her hair drenched in sweat? Roller derby retailers are one step ahead of the game, and many derby-style accessories such as leopard-print bow hairclips complete with roller skate charms are now available, while bandanas and hairbands are also used to cover the post-practice sweaty-betty bonce.

Quadratic Abrasion of the Apocalypstix, Atlanta Rollergirls, USA. Photo by Timothy Moxley.

Short back and sides: Racey Slam Hard, London Rollergirls, make-up by Louise O'Neill and Erica Schlegel. Photo by Danny Bourne.

Chopper Bleed of the Toxic Shocks, Atlanta Rollergirls, USA. Photo by Timothy Moxley.

Sinister smile: Rettig to Rumble of the Rat City Rollergirls, USA. Photo by Jules Doyle.

MAKE-UP

If you think the hairstyles are creative, they are nothing compared to the make-up. In roller derby, make-up is used as war paint, a device to intimidate your opponents and freak people out. War paint is make-up traditionally used in some tribal societies, to decorate the face and body before battle. In roller derby, many different make-up styles are found on the track, but the overall desired effect is often the same: to distort the face and shock the opposition. Many rollergirls have a signature make-up look. For example, legendary heavy metal band KISS-style make-up is worn by Betty Ford Galaxy of the Rat City Rollergirls from Seattle, USA. Her face is masked with a white base, and adorned with batwing-style eyes outlined in black and filled in with silver. This is where Krista Williams is left at home and Betty Ford Galaxy is born.

Many girls go for a deathly look with a white base and black eyes, sometimes with skeleton-style detail. However, the most creative looks

In roller derby, make-up is used as war paint, a device to intimidate your opponents and freak people out.

are those that distort the structure of the face's anatomy. Dr Rock of the Royal Windsor Rollergirls in the UK does this particularly well, accentuating her big blue eyes with heavy black eyeliner, and painting on two more sets of mutant eyes underneath to give the effect of a six-eyed creature, then accentuating her lips into a sharp pout. Many girls go for a 'half face' look, distorting the features on half the face by enlarging the mouth on one side, as shown by Rettig to Rumble of the Rat City Rollergirls. Demanda Riot of the Bay Area Rollergirls is known for her signature look with a white base all over the face and a black visor-style stripe across her eyes. Frak Attack, formerly of Castle Rock'N'Rollers and now with Rocky Mountain Roller Girls, can be seen sporting a variety of make-up styles, including the cyborg-style half-woman, half-robot, among others. Make-up is often co-ordinated with uniforms, and sometimes a whole team will participate in a make-up theme. It can be the perfect finishing touch to a boutfit.

Half-woman, half-robot: Frak Attack formerly of Castle Rock N Rollers now with Rocky Mountain Rollergirls, USA. Photo by Amanda Renee, Wicked Shamrock Photography.

Day of the dead: Ceecee Slammer of Leeds Roller Dolls, UK. Photo by Jason Ruffell.

War paint: Betty Ford Galaxy of the Rat City Rollergirls and Demanda Riot of the Bay Area Derby Girls, USA. Photo by Jules Doyle.

All eyes on you: Dr Rock of the
Royal Windsor Rollergirls, UK.
Photo by Jason Ruffell.

Lady in red: Red N Roll of the London Rockin' Rollers, UK. Make-up by Louise O'Neill and Erica Schlegel. Photo by Danny Bourne.

Bloody Valentine of the London Rockin' Rollers, UK. Make up by Louise O'Neill and Erica Schlegel. Photo by Danny Bourne.

Jeopardy Jinx of Croydon Roller Derby, UK. Make-up by Louise O'Neill and Erica Schlegel. Photo by Danny Bourne.

Demanda Riot of the Bay Area
Derby Girls, USA. Photo by Jules
Doyle.

TATTOOS

There is a lot of awesome ink on display both on and off the track. The tattoos go with the look and many derby girls and guys can be seen embellished with creative designs of all kinds. There are many different reasons that people choose to have tattoos. People use tattoos to create narratives, to represent personal choices they have made, to illustrate their biographies, and to demonstrate their personal, political and cultural values to others.

Tattooing is a way to enhance and demonstrate individuality. Being heavily tattooed can give a person a very individual look, but can also mean that person is associated with a group identity. Being heavily tattooed is still outside of social norms so people with tattoos are often associated with a certain lifestyle. Many of these people are perceived as deviant and attempting to undermine the dominant order. This is all related to punk and alternative music subcultures, which, of course, played a big part in the origins of the current roller derby revival. Austin, Texas has one of the most prominent alternative music scenes in the world and is famed for the slogan 'Keep Austin Weird'.

Full- and half-sleeve tattoos are favoured by many a rollergirl, and some have tattoos especially dedicated to the sport. There are quite a few rollergirls with skates, wheels, team names and logos inked onto their skin – they are rollergirls and proud of it, and display their tattoos as a testament to that pride and their love of the sport. Some skaters even have portraits of their rollergirl personas emblazoned along the lengths of their arms, or representations of their own beloved skates as well as scrolls scripted with the words 'roller derby' professing their love of the sport as a way of life. Even the infamous Ann Calvello could be seen flashing some ink around the rink.

Awesome ink: Beat Down Barbie, formerly of Castle Rock N Rollers, USA. Photo by Amanda Renee, Wicked Shamrock Photography.

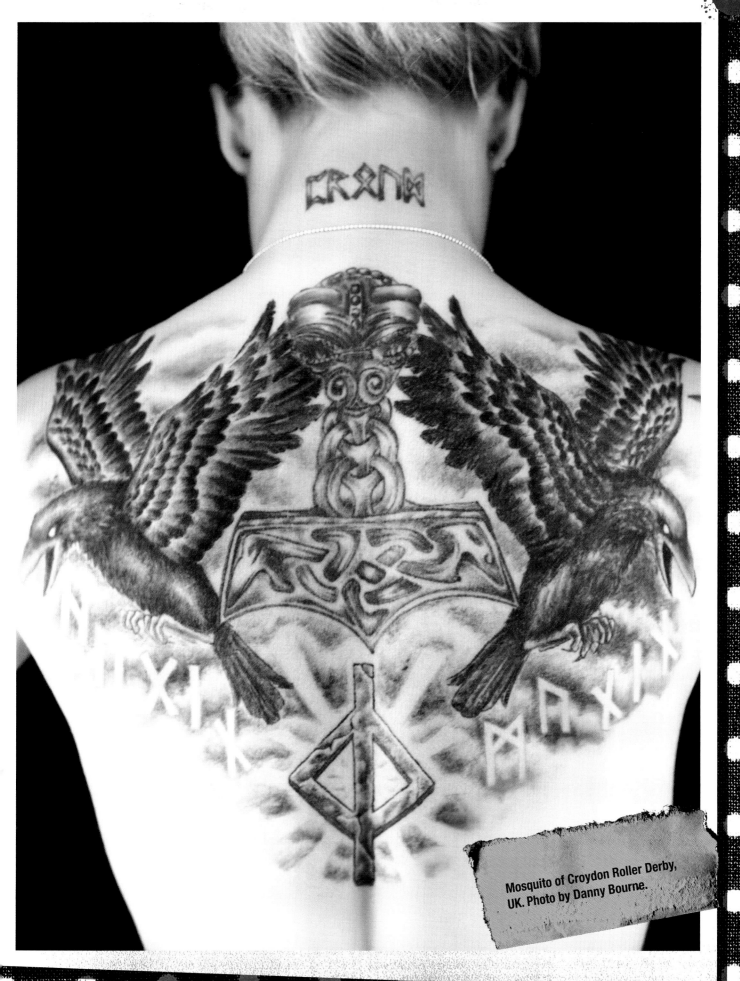

Mosquito of Croydon Roller Derby, UK. Photo by Danny Bourne.

Bubbles von Vieux of Big Easy Rollergirls, USA. Photo by Akoch Photography, LLC. © 2011.

That's dedication: Lucy-fur Brawl of the Mississippi Rollergirls, USA, with her derby name tattooed across her chest. Photo by Akoch Photography , LLC. © 2011.

Sm'Hittin of the Mississippi Rollergirls, USA. Photo by Akoch Photography, LLC. © 2011.

Katy Peril of the Ultraviolent
Femmes, London Rollergirls, UK.
Photo by Danny Bourne.

INTERVIEW WITH DOM HOLMES: THE FAMILY BUSINESS, LONDON, UK

Dom Holmes, The Family Business, UK.

HOW AND WHY DID YOU BECOME A TATTOO ARTIST?

I decided when I got my first tattoo that it was what I wanted to do. I was only 15 at the time, which I don't condone, but as soon as I got a tattoo, everything about it was what I wanted to do. I had always been fascinated by tattoos anyway. As soon as I got tattooed, I started thinking about how I could become a tattoo artist myself. I started gearing everything in my life to work towards becoming a tattoo artist: I got more tattoos, did a lot of drawing, spoke to a lot of different people and asked for any advice that I could. It was while I was at university in Manchester when a friend helped me to get everything I needed together to start tattooing, and it was from there that I managed to get my first job in a tattoo studio in Macclesfield in 2002.

DO YOU HAVE A SPECIALIST STYLE, AND IF SO, HOW DID YOU DEVELOP IT?

I suppose my style is quite difficult to pinpoint. My work is influenced by Far-Eastern art, not just Japanese but also Tibetan styles of painting. I also use a lot of Mehndi pattern work and I like the really ornate decorative styles from that part of the world, but obviously, having spent the majority of my life in this country, my work has a very Western style to it too. I'd say it's really a fusion of East and West. But I find with my style I take on a lot of different sorts of work image-wise. I like to take on new things and do something that's a bit different that I haven't done before. In terms of how it develops, if you ask any tattoo artist, your style is something that develops naturally. Not many people get into tattooing and straightaway decide that all their tattoos will be traditional Japanese or Sailor Jerry. As your artwork develops, your tattooing develops and your style finds you in a way – it's an organic process that develops as you go along. A lot of artists are selective about what work they do, but even if they do a lot of similar types of tattoos, their own style will come through within that subject matter anyway.

As soon as I got a tattoo, everything about it was what I wanted to do.

HOW DID YOU DEVELOP YOUR INTEREST IN EASTERN STYLES? IS IT SOMETHING YOU STUDIED OR CAME ACROSS WHEN TRAVELLING?

I think it started when I was at art college. I instantly had an attraction to those styles of art, and it has influenced everything I've done since

then – my painting and drawing as well as tattooing. I've always thought back to those styles and tried to emulate them. I think it must come from then, from seeing something and straightaway feeling such a connection.

ARE YOU STILL PAINTING AND DRAWING NOW?

I do as much painting and drawing as I have time to do. I also do a lot of illustration and design work outside of tattooing, such as book covers and clothing design.

TATTOOS ARE PART OF AN ALTERNATIVE SUBCULTURE. DO YOU THINK THEY GIVE PEOPLE MORE OF AN INDIVIDUAL IDENTITY OR MORE OF A GROUP IDENTITY?

I think people who are tattooed know their own identity and know where they fit in and feel very much that the tattoos they have are for them and feel individual, but it's different for people who don't have tattoos. I think a lot of society still sees people with tattoos in the same way. People still take one look at me and assume that all I listen to is punk rock and that I hang out in certain places, and they form an opinion of me very quickly based on the fact that I have tattoos, and are very surprised when I don't fit into that mould. But other people who have tattoos would not straightaway make those assumptions about me. It's a sort of divide between the people who don't know very much about it and then the people who have had a bit of an experience with it and are aware of tattoo culture. They see it differently.

MANY ROLLER DERBY SKATERS HAVE TATTOOS. WHY DO YOU THINK IT'S PART OF THE CULTURE ASSOCIATED WITH THE SPORT?

A lot of rollergirls are very strong, ballsy, loud people so maybe the tattoos fit them and their personalities. It's all part of asserting your

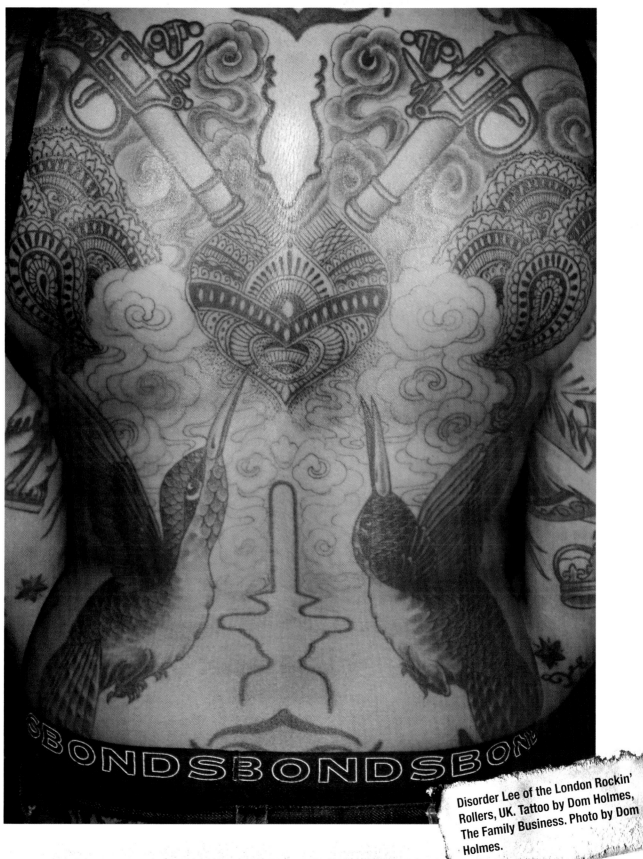

SBONDSBONDSBON

Disorder Lee of the London Rockin' Rollers, UK. Tattoo by Dom Holmes, The Family Business. Photo by Dom Holmes.

personality on the world, and the tattoos are a way for them to express who they are and make themselves seen and heard. That's the only thing I can think of, but it is a strange thing that it has attracted a lot of tattooed people. Both of these are offshoots of the punk culture which is a big part of the tattoo community but tattooing has become part of lots of different cultures and groups of people that you can't account for. A completely opposite extreme is footballers now – they all have tattoos and the same sort of tattoos – it's strange to see a footballer without tattoos now.

HOW MANY ROLLERGIRLS HAVE YOU TATTOOED AND WHICH WAS THE MOST SIGNIFICANT?

I've tattooed quite a few, a lot of them just drop it into conversation. One girl I used to tattoo has moved to Wales recently, but she got really, really into roller derby and she had a lot of tattoos, but I think she got less tattoos the more she got into the sport because of the risk of falling down and getting hurt. One of my favourite customers started doing roller derby fairly recently and she is very heavily tattooed. When she first started getting tattoos, she just got one or two but now she's so covered. She's a very strong, beautiful woman, she's 5ft 10 and she's black, but

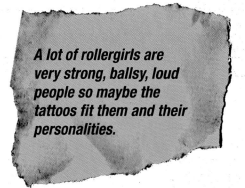

A lot of rollergirls are very strong, ballsy, loud people so maybe the tattoos fit them and their personalities.

there aren't that many black girls who do the sport. In a way she's your typical rollergirl: she's very loud and bolshy and is the kind of person I'd expect to do it actually. Most of the rollergirls I've tattooed have tattoos with meanings, but Lee [Disorder Lee, London Rockin' Rollers] just likes to be tattooed because she likes the way it looks.

WHAT PARTICULAR TRENDS IN TATTOO STYLES HAVE YOU NOTICED AMONG ROLLERGIRLS?

I'd say there are a lot of traditional tattoos like hearts and roses and swallows, quite a lot of vintage styles. That's what I've been asked to do by rollergirls, and it sort of goes with a lot of those other subcultures like the burlesque and the rockabilly styles that go with the sport. But I find it quite interesting that someone like Lee [Disorder Lee, London Rockin' Rollers] has started doing roller derby because she's not rockabilly or vintage, she's just quite tomboyish, not really dressed up at all and just has her own style. Her tattoos are a different style from a lot of the other rollergirls I've tattooed.

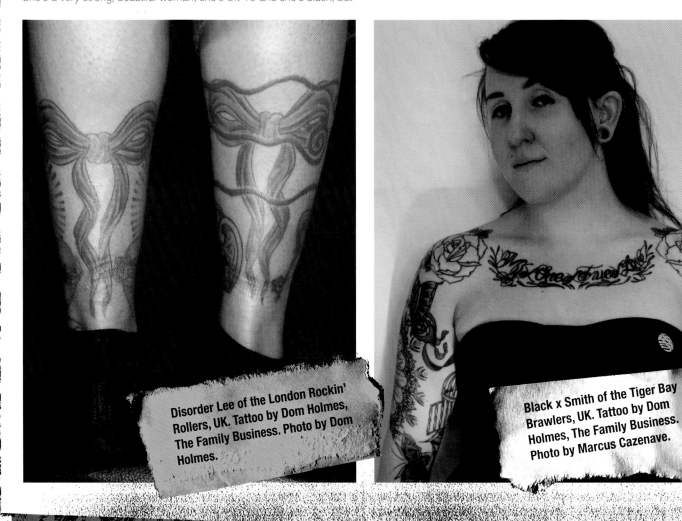

Disorder Lee of the London Rockin' Rollers, UK. Tattoo by Dom Holmes, The Family Business. Photo by Dom Holmes.

Black x Smith of the Tiger Bay Brawlers, UK. Tattoo by Dom Holmes, The Family Business. Photo by Marcus Cazenave.

HAVE YOU EVER BEEN ASKED TO TATTOO SOMEONE WITH THEIR ROLLER DERBY NAME OR TEAM LOGO?
I never have but I think I would definitely do that if someone asked me. It's possible that I have tattooed someone's roller derby name without knowing what it was, but I think I would know because I do usually ask about the significance of any names. I think that would be very cool because it is something that they love and it takes up a big part of their lives so they are obviously very passionate about it.

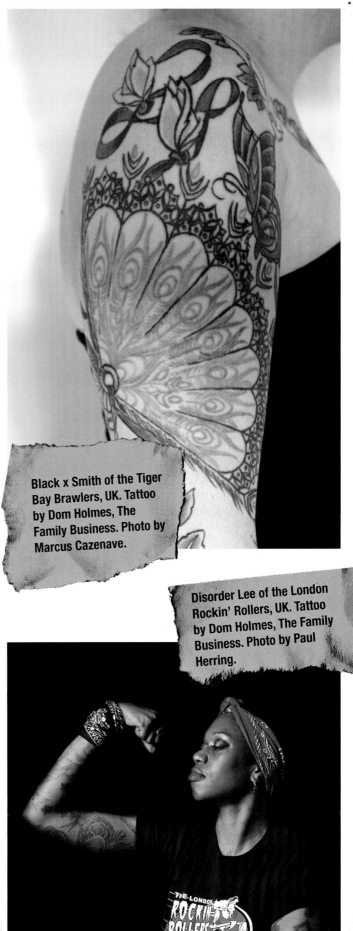

Black x Smith of the Tiger Bay Brawlers, UK. Tattoo by Dom Holmes, The Family Business. Photo by Marcus Cazenave.

Disorder Lee of the London Rockin' Rollers, UK. Tattoo by Dom Holmes, The Family Business. Photo by Paul Herring.

Black x Smith of the Tiger Bay Brawlers, UK. Tattoo by Dom Holmes, The Family Business. Photo by Marcus Cazenave.

GLOSSARY

25 laps A speed test that involves skating 25 laps in 5 minutes.

Arm check A shoulder-to-shoulder contact hit.

Back block Where a skater hits another skater in the back.

Blocker Defensive skater position. Blockers set up plays to help their jammer or block the opposing jammer.

Boot camp An intensive roller derby training session that can last up to several days.

Bout A roller derby tournament or game is referred to as a bout. A bout is usually broken up into two 30-minute halves, and those halves are broken up into two-minute races called jams.

Boutfits Outfits worn by the skaters during bouts.

Call off The lead jammer can call off or cancel the jam at any time.

Crossover Crossing one foot over the other when skating to aid acceleration.

Cut track Crossing the infield to rejoin the pack after you fall.

Forearms Blocking illegally using the elbows.

Derby stop A stop involving turning around and stopping on the toe stops of the skates.

Duck runs A method of running on skates where the toes are pushed outwards and the skater picks up their feet in order to aid acceleration.

Ellipsis The fastest route around an oval track.

Four-point fall A safe method of falling where the skater falls onto their shins, knees and forearms.

Fresh Meat New skaters.

Helmet Panties Helmet covers worn by the jammer and pivot to identify their positions.

Hip whip When one player pulls on another player's hips to aid acceleration round the track.

Hit To block using full contact.

Inside line The interior line of the track.

Inside whip Where one player assists another to accelerate around the inside of the track.

Jammer Scoring skater position designated by a star on her helmet. Her objective is to score one point per opposing blocker she laps.

Lead jammer The jammer who breaks through the pack first and the only one that can call off a jam.

Leg whip When one player uses their outstretched leg to whip another player round the track and gain speed.

Minimum skills A specific skill requirement established by WFTDA and OSDA. These are the minimum skating, gameplay and rule-knowledge skills a skater must possess before they can play competitively.

One-knee fall A safe method of falling onto one knee so that a fast recovery can be made and a skater can get up quickly.

Outside line The exterior line of the track.

Outside whip Where one player assists another to accelerate around the outside of the track.

Pack A group of skaters, four from each team. This includes three blockers and one pivot. The pack skates together (most leagues require that they stay within 20 feet of each other) and their goal is to ensure that their team's jammer is helped through the pack while preventing the opposing team's jammer from getting through.

Pad stink The smell of sweaty knee and elbow pads.

Penalty box A designated area where skaters who have committed one major or four minor penalties are sent to sit out for one minute.

Pivot Defensive skater position designated by a stripe down the middle of her helmet and known as the front pacesetter for the pack.

Plough A method of stopping on skates where legs are wide apart with the heels turned out.

Positional blocking Blocking opposing players without hitting.

Scrimmage A practice game that isn't open to the public.

Star pass When the jammer passes her helmet panty to the pivot, who then takes over as jammer.

Toe-stop run Running on the toe stops of the skates in order to build up speed.

T stop Dragging the back skate perpendicular to the front skate in order to stop.

Two-knee fall A safe method of falling onto two knees so that a fast recovery can be made and a skater can get up quickly.

Waitress whip A fancy type of whip where one player spins around and stops in order to pull the other player around her to aid acceleration.

Whips An assist move in which a skater extends her arm and whips her jammer around the track, propelling her with momentum.

Zebra Referees and NSOs are referred to as zebras because of their black and white uniforms.

Zombie fairy Taking tiny steps picking both feet up off the ground while wearing skates.

FURTHER READING AND OTHER RESOURCES

BOOKS

Jennifer Barbee and Alex Cohen, *Down and Derby: The Insider's Guide to Roller Derby* (Soft Skull Press, 2010).
This is a great beginner's guide to the sport. It explains everything you need to know if you are thinking about playing roller derby, from the history to the rules, skates and protective gear, as well as how to join a league and info on referees. This book covers all the basics for getting started.

Toni Carr, *Knockdown Knits* (John Wiley & Sons, 2008).
This is one of my favourites. The Naptown Roller Girls of Indianapolis, Indiana share the patterns they use when they're knitting in the off-time. Full of roller derby-inspired knitting patterns, this book features 30 fab knitting projects for all levels.

Keith Coppage, *Roller Derby to Rollerjam: The Authorized Story of an Unauthorized Sport* (Santa Rosa, California: Squarebooks, 1999).
Keith Coppage is one of the original roller derby photographers from back in the sport's original heyday. Another great book for researching the history of roller derby.

Shauna Cross, *Derby Girl* (Henry Holt, 2007)
Written by the LA Derby Dolls' former skater Shauna Cross, aka Maggie Mayhem, *Derby Girl* is the novel on which *Whip It*, the derby film skaters all know and love, was based. It tells the story of teenager Bliss Cavendar's escape from her small-town life through her discovery of the exciting world of roller derby in Austin, Texas.

Frank Deford, *Five Strides on the Banked Track: The Life and Times of the Roller Derby* (Little Brown & Company, 1971).
Written during the 1970s, this is a real eye-opener to the history of the sport. Written in an archaic, often hilarious and unmistakably male voice, the book is an account of the history of roller derby up until 1971. It pays particular attention to roller derby's historic star players such as Anne Calvello and Joan Weston.

Jim Fitzpatrick, *Roller Derby Classics ... and more!* (Trafford Publishing, 2005)
Former professional Roller Derby skater, referee, photographer and fan, Jim Fitzpatrick spent years compiling a huge collection of memorabilia of the original Roller Derby, and this book is the sum of his collection. Includes a foreword by Ann Calvello and many rare and never-before-seen photos.

Melissa Joulwan, *Rollergirl: Totally True Tales from the Track,* (Touchstone Books, 2007).
This book is the personal story of one of the revival's original rollergirls, Melissa (aka Meliscious) Joulwan. She writes the story of the formation of the first women's flat-track league in Texas, their split into two leagues and the establishment of other leagues that followed in quick succession across the US, the development of WFTDA and the establishment of the sport as we know it today. A great introduction to roller derby and full of great stories.

Catherine Mabe, *Roller Derby: The History and All-Girl Revival of the Greatest Sport on Wheels* (Speck Press, 2007)
Another great introduction to the recent roller derby revival, including a foreword by derby legend Ivanna S. Pankin. This is one of the best contemporary illustrated books on roller derby out there.

Herb Michelson, *A Very Simple Game: the Story of Roller Derby* (Occasional Pub. Co., 1971)
A history of roller derby written some 40 years ago.

Pamela Ribon, *Going in Circles* (Downtown Press, 2010)
Another novel embracing the subject of roller derby. *Going in Circles* tells the story of Charlotte Goodman who, suffering from severe

anxiety during the breakup of her marriage, finds salvation in roller derby after being introduced to the sport by a friend.

MAGAZINES

Blood and Thunder Magazine
http://www.bloodandthundermag.com/

fiveonfive
http://fiveonfivemag.com/

Fracture
http://www.fracturemag.com/

FILM

Roller Derby Girl, (1949). A 10-minute short film produced and directed by Justin Herman was released as part of Paramount's *Pacemaker* series.

Derby (titled **Roller Derby** in the UK), (1971). Directed by Robert Kaylor and produced by Jerry Seltzer's own company, the film follows skater Mike Snell as he becomes immersed in the world of 1970s professional roller derby, and provides competition footage as well as a behind-the-scenes look at the lives of several roller derby pros.

Roller Derby Mania (1986). This 57-minute documentary was released direct to video (NTSC VHS) in North America. It features the L.A. T-Birds Roller Games team, and includes archival footage of the game's previous incarnations.

Roller Derby Wars was released direct to video (NTSC VHS) in North America. It was released on video in the UK in 1993.

The Fireball (1950) is the story of a boy, played by Mickey Rooney, who runs away to join the roller derby.

Unholy Rollers: The Leader of the Pack (1972) The tale of a woman who quits her job to start a new life as a rollergirl.

Kansas City Bomber (1972) starring the fabulous Raquel Welch as a derby girl rising to fame.

Demon of the Derby: The Ann Calvello Story (2001) tells the story of one of derby's all-time greats, Ann Calvello.

Jam (2006) is a film about the lives of derby skaters and promoters in Texas.

High Heels on Wheels (2006) A film featuring several former professional skaters reminiscing about their roles as female athletes and 'out' lesbians in the roller derby community.

Rollergirls (2006) is a series of 13 hour-long reality-style episodes about roller derby in Texas.

Hell-on-Wheels: The True Tale of All-Girl Roller Derby, Texas Style (2007) A documentary about the beginnings of women's roller derby in Texas.

Blood on the Flat Track (2007) A documentary about the formation of Seattle's Rat City Rollergirls, it premiered at the 2007 Seattle International Film Festival.

Roller Derby Revival (2008) A short feature about the roller derby revival.

Roller Derby Dolls (2008) A short documentary about the recent revival of roller derby in Australia.

Roller Warriors is a 7-part documentary series covering the 2008 Kansas City Roller Warriors season.

Speed Queen (2009) The 'Speed Queen' is Ulrike Kubatta, video artist and a former motorcycle courier, who briefly swapped the hazardous streets of central London for the fast and frenzied world of the American sport of roller derby.

Whip It (2009) An adaptation of former La Derby Doll Shauna Cross's novel starring Ellen Page ('Juno') as Bliss Cavendar, an indie-rock-loving misfit of Bodeen, Texas, where football and beauty pageants are the guiding lights. Still, she finds a way of dealing with her small-town misery by discovering a roller derby league in nearby Austin.

Brutal Beauty: Tales of the Rose City Rollers (2010) is a recent documentary about a league in Portland, Oregon.

Star Cross'd Jammers (2011). A romantic comedy blended with roller derby action. It combines a modern-day sport with a classic Shakespearian tale. A Romeo and Juliet-style feud between two roller derby leagues that despise one another is further enraged when the star jammers from each league fall in love.

Derby Baby (2011). Emmy-winning filmmakers Robin Bond and Dave Wruck take you along on their quest to learn why women's flat track roller derby is the most controversial and fastest growing sport in the world.

SUPPLIERS

ROLLER DERBY CLOTHING

Beserk Clothing
http://www.beserkclothing.com/roller-derby

Broken Cherry
http://www.brokencherry.com/

Café Press (roller derby gifts)
http://shop.cafepress.co.uk/roller-derby

Derbyliscious
http://derbylicious.com/

Derby or Die
http://store.derbyordie.com/

Derby Little Secrets
http://www.derbylittlesecrets.com

Derby Owned
http://www.derbyowned.com

Derby Skinz
http://derbyskinz.com/

Deviant Derby
http://www.deviantderby.com/

Dolled Up Derby
http://www.dolledupderby.com/

Dress Derby
http://www.dressderby.com

Free Radicals HQ
http://www.freeradicalshq.com/

Gothabillys
http://www.gothabillys.com

Opus Oils (roller derby perfume)
http://opusoils.com/page9.html

Pivotstar
http://pivotstar.com

Roller Derby Shirts
https://rollerderbyshirts.com/

Skate Asylum
http://www.skateasylum.co.uk

Skulls and Rainbows
http://www.skullsandrainbows.com/

Tatty Divine
http://www.tattydevine.com/boutique/index.php

Team Colours UK (bespoke uniforms)
http://www.team-colours.co.uk/roller-derby/

Wicked Skatewear
http://wickedskatewear.com/

SKATES, PADS AND OTHER KIT

Atom Wheels
http://www.atomwheels.com/

Bones Bearings
http://www.bonesbearings.com/

Billy's
http://www.billys.co.uk/

Connie's Skate Place
http://www.create-a-skate.com/

Cruz Skate Shop
http://cruzskateshop.com/

Emerald City Skates
http://www.emeraldcityskates.com/

Everglides
http://www.everglides.co.uk/

Fast Girl Skates
http://www.fastgirlskates.com/

Just Skates
http://www.justskates.com/

Low Price Skates
http://www.lowpriceskates.com/

Net Skate
http://www.netskate.com/

New Skates
http://www.newskates.com/

Planet on Wheels
http://www.planetonwheels.com/

Pro Designed
http://www.prodesigned.com/

Proline Skates
http://www.prolineskates.com (UK)

Pro-Tec
http://www.pro-tec.net/

Radar Wheels
http://www.radarwheels.com/

Riedell
http://www.riedellskates.com/

Rocky Mountain Skates
http://www.shop.rockymountainskates.com/

Roller Derby Depot
http://www.rollerderbydepot.com/

Roller Derby Shop
http://www.rollerderbyshop.com/

Roller Derby Virginia Beach
http://www.rollerderbyvb.com/

Rollergirl Skates
http://www.rollergirlskates.com/

RollerGirl.CA
http://www.rollergirl.ca/

Roller Guy Skates
http://www.rollerguyskates.com/

Sin City Skates
http://sincityskates.com/

Skate Attack
http://www.skateattack.co.uk/

Skaterbros
http://skaterbros.com/

Skate Buys
http://www.skate-buys.com/

Skates.com
http://www.skates.com/

Skatemail
http://www.skatemall.com/

Skates n Such
http://www.skatesnsuch.com/

Smiths Scabs
http://www.smithsafetygear.com/

Sure Grip
http://www.suregrip.com/

TSG
http://www.ridetsg.com/

Vanilla Skates
http://www.vanillaskates.com/

Via Derby
http://www.viaderby.com/

XSports Protective
http://www.xsportsprotective.com/

USEFUL WEBSITES

WFTDA
http://wftda.com/

Two Evils
http://www.twoevils.org/rollergirls/

Roller Derby Worldwide
http://www.derbyroster.com/

Old School Derby Association
http://osda.us/

UK Roller Derby Association
http://ukrda.org.uk/

Men's Roller Derby Association
http://www.mensderbycoalition.com/

Derbalife
http://derbalife.blogspot.com/

European Roller Derby Central
http://www.euroderby.org/

Roller Derby Workout
http://www.rollerderbyworkout.com/

Roller Derby Foundation
http://www.rollerderbyfoundation.org/

Derby News Network
http://www.derbynewsnetwork.com/

Museum of Roller Skating
http://www.rollerskatingmuseum.com/

BLOGS/SOCIAL NETWORKS

Roller Derby Girls
http://www.rollerderbygirls.org/

Roller Derby Quilt
http://www.rollerderbyquilt.com/

Live Derby Girls
http://livederbygirls.com/

Yo Roller Derby
http://www.yorollerderby.com/

Derby Girl
http://derbygirlblog.com/

Secret Diary of a Rookie Rollergirl
http://secretdiaryofarookierollergirl.wordpress.com/

Derby Girls Blog
http://derbygirlsblog.com/

Queen of the Rink
http://www.queenoftherink.com/

EVENTS

Rollercon
http://rollercon.net/

The Big 5 WFTDA Tournaments
http://wftda.com/The-Big-5

WFTDA Events
http://wftda.com/events

Roller Derby World Cup
http://www.bloodandthundermag.com/WorldCup2011.htm